Old-Fashioned Recipes For Modern Cooks

Foods With All The Flavor You Remember In Grandmother's Cooking

AdvanceBooks
Houston, Texas, USA
www.advancebooks.com

OLD-FASHIONED RECIPES FOR MODERN COOKS
Copyright © 2001 by L.B. Cobb. All rights reserved.

No part of this book may be reproduced or transmitted in any form or by any means, electronic or mechanical, including photocopying, recording, or by any information storage and retrieval system, without written permission from the publisher, except as brief quotations embodied in critical articles and reviews. Contact ADVANCEBOOKS by email at staff@advancebooks.com for information on rights.

ADVANCEBOOKS

AN IMPRINT OF
ADVANCE BOOKS COMPANY
Houston, TX, USA
www.advancebooks.com
staff@advancebooks.com

Library of Congress Control Number
2001096515
ISBN 0-9706224-0-6

First Trade Paper Printing
November 2001
10 9 8 7 6 5 4 3 2 1

Printed on acid-free paper
Manufactured in the United States of America

This cookbook is dedicated to Martha Wilson, Edith Burkhart, and Kathryne Cobb, who generously shared their family recipes, and to Clara Nixon Dawson (1902-1998) and Linnie Belle Henegar Snodderly (1885-1974), who gave treasured memories while nourishing bodies and souls.

The compiler and editor of this cookbook, LB Cobb, is an attorney who grew up in Tennessee, practiced geology then law, and now plays with grandchildren and writes. Her first novel, *Splendor Bay*, will be published in December 2001. She and her husband live in Houston, Texas.

INTRODUCTION

Old-Fashioned Recipes for Modern Cooks was inspired by a dinner-table conversation. What else?

My good friend Martha Wilson recently developed a "food fetish"—she can't live without the Food Channel. Practicing her new-found culinary skills, Martha had prepared one of her mother's Tex-Mex recipes. Talk turned to other dishes Clara Nixon Dawson, a native-born and lifelong Texan, had made for us over the years, then to other soul-satisfying foods we have tasted at other tables and how we wished we had the recipes.

Weeks later, Martha came across her mother's recipes, some dating from the World War I era when Clara, then a teenager, "kept house" for her father, brothers and sisters after her own mother died. Then I visited my mother, Edith Burkhart, a lifelong East Tennessean now in her eighties, and insisted she reveal her own and my grandmother's, Linnie Belle Henegar Snodderly's, kitchen secrets. I also quizzed my Mississippi-born octogenarian mother-in-law, Kathryne Moore Cobb, about the delicious foods I've eaten at her table over the years.

That's how *Old-Fashioned Recipes for Modern Cooks* came into being. It contains over 175 Southern and Southwestern dishes from the days before "fat-free"—wonderful breakfast, lunch, and dinner foods our mothers and grandmothers prepared routinely but we tend to ignore while reading calorie- and fat-grams off microwave food labels. And desserts. Cake recipes begin on page 29, pie recipes on page 36, cookies on page 46, and other deserts on page 50.

And that brings me to the first word of caution. If you're determined to count fat-grams and calories, you should probably put this book back on the shelf and walk away right now. None of these recipes will give you that information. Or you might take note that Clara Dawson lived to age 96 and Belle Snodderly lived almost 90 years and neither of them ever counted a fat-gram or calorie, or jogged, either.

Of course, it's possible to do as I often do—read these recipes and imagine the taste of real food while zapping something "lite" in the microwave. The "fillet of fish" I just pulled from my freezer zaps in six minutes and has such wonderful ingredients as hydrogenated vegetable oil, cellulose gel, tripolyphosphate, citric acid, cellulose gum, hydrolyzed corn protein, and BHA and BHT preservatives, but only 90 calories per serving and a money-back guarantee. Yum! Yum!

On the plus side, these recipes don't have to be followed rigidly. They've been handed down for generations with each cook adding and subtracting a bit of this and a handful of that to make it their own. If you think a dish needs a dash of this or a pinch of that, or even a lot of something else to make it taste right, then throw it in. Experiment. It's your taste buds you're trying to satisfy. If it works, you have a new family recipe. If it doesn't, you'll know better next time.

I've provided hints where special care needs to be exercised, the first being to calibrate your oven temperature on the first batch of anything you bake. Modern, tightly-insulated ovens may cook "faster" than older recipes indicate. When canning or preserving foods, always use sterile (scalded clean) jars. For the best results, use fresh ingredients. I know it's hard to come by just-churned butter, eggs straight from the hen house, creamy milk that came from a cow this morning, or vegetables plucked from the backyard garden. Do the best you can.

And, when you're in the midst of one of these recipes, peeling, chopping, kneading, stirring, or whisking away, remember our mothers and grandmothers cooked like this for large families—three square meals every day and an extra big after-church dinner for extended family and visitors on Sunday—with no food-processor, no dishwasher, and no air-conditioning in their houses. Then be grateful you have a fast food place down the street where you can get a bucket of something made with secret ingredients when a crowd appears on your doorstep!

L.B. Cobb

OLD-FASHIONED RECIPES FOR MODERN COOKS

TABLE OF CONTENTS

Note: Clara Dawson's recipes are identified by (CD), Martha Wilson's by (MW), Linnie Belle Snodderly's by (LS), Edith Burkhart's by (EB), Kathryne Cobb's by (KC), and LB Cobb's by (LC).

Page	
1	**BISCUITS & BREADS**
1	Buttermilk Biscuits (LS)
2	Biscuit Gravy (LS)
3	Plain Biscuits (LS)
3	Biscuit Variations (LS)
4	Cornbread (KC)
4	Buttermilk Cornbread (EB)
5	Pinches/Mexican Corn Muffins (CD)
5	Cornbread Variations (CD)
6	Bran Muffins (KC)
6	Easy Nut Bread (CD)
7	Waffles (KC)
7	Pop Overs (KC)
8	Sweet Rolls or Coffee Cake (CD)
8	Sourdough Bread (KC)
10	Sourdough Biscuits (KC)
10	Potato Muffins (EB)
11	**MAIN COURSE**
11	**Chicken**
11	Chicken and Dumplings (LS)
12	Southern Fried Chicken (EB)
12	Fried Chicken Gravy (EB)
12	Diet Chicken (MW)
13	Curry Chicken (CD)
13	Chicken-Green Bean Casserole (CD)
14	Chicken Baked in Wine (MW)
14	King Ranch Chicken (CD)
15	Chicken Spaghetti (CD)
16	Chicken Parmesan (KC)
16	Chicken Salad Mold (CD)

17	**Other Poultry**
17	Roast Duck (CD)
17	Roast Quail (CD)
18	Roast Turkey (EB)
18	Oyster Stuffing (EB)
19	Giblet Gravy (EB)
20	Mushroom Nut Stuffing (CD)
20	Chestnut Stuffing (CD)
21	**Seafood**
21	Gumbo (CD)
21	Creamed Tuna (CD)
22	Salmon Croquettes (CD)
22	Flaked Fish Casserole (KC)
23	Scalloped Oysters (CD)
23	Fish Fritters (KC)
24	**Meats**
24	Meat Loaf (EB)
24	Stuffed Green Peppers (KC)
25	Roast Beef (KC)
25	Sausage and Onion Casserole (LC)
26	Chili (CD)
26	Chili with Beans (CD)
27	Pork Chops with Apple Stuffing (KC)
27	Barbecued Ribs (LC)
28	Sweet and Sour Pork Chops (CD)
28	Liver and Onions (LC)
29	**DESSERTS**
29	**Cakes**
29	Grandma's Cake-Making Instructions
30	Grandma's Yellow Cake (LS)
31	Spice Cake (LS)
31	Nut Cake (LS)
31	Fudge Cake (LS)
31	Banana Cake (EB)
32	Grandma's Devil's Food Cake (LS)
33	Gingerbread (CD)
33	Apricot-Nut Bread (CD)
34	**Icings**
34	Fluffy Boiled Icing (LS)

OLD-FASHIONED RECIPES/TABLE OF CONTENTS

35 Fluffy Chocolate Icing (LS)
35 Chocolate Topping (LS)
35 Creamy Butter Icing (CD)
36 Chocolate Icing (CD)
36 **Tarts & Patties**
36 **Pie**
37 Grandma's Pie Crust Instructions
38 Plain Pie Pastry (LS)
39 Buttermilk Pie (CD)
39 Pecan Pie (KC)
40 Apple Pie (EB)
40 Meringue (KC)
41 Lemon Meringue Pie (KC)
41 Key Lime Pie (KC)
42 Custard Pie (EB)
42 Coconut Custard Pie (EB)
43 Sweet Potato Pie (LS)
43 Pumpkin Pie (EB)
44 Blackberry Pie (EB)
44 Blueberry Pie (KC)
45 Rhubarb Pie (KC)
45 Green Tomato Pie (CD)
46 **Cookies**
46 Sugar Cookies (CD)
47 Peanut Butter Cookies (CD)
47 Old-Fashioned Oatmeal Cookies (CD)
47 Orange Oatmeal Cookies (CD)
48 Cathedral Cookies (CD)
48 Christmas Cookies (CD)
49 Orange No-Bake Cookies (CD)
50 **Other Desserts**
50 Pineapple Sherbet (CD)
50 Fruit-Gelatin Salad (KC)
51 Pink Arctic Mold (CD)
51 Baked Custard (EB)
51 Banana Pudding (EB)
52 Easy Fudge (LC)
52 Buttermilk Fudge (KC)
53 Pecan Pralines (KC)

OLD-FASHIONED RECIPES/TABLE OF CONTENTS

54   Quick Spiced Peaches (EB)
54   Quick Peach Cobbler (EB)
55   **SOUPS**
55   Asparagus Soup (CD)
55   Bean Soup (EB)
56   Clam Chowder (LC)
56   Manhattan Clam Chowder (LC)
56   Cream of Tomato Soup (CD)
57   Corn Chowder (KC)
57   Cream of Onion Soup (KC)
58   Chicken Soup (CD)
58   Simple Vegetable Soup (KC)
59   Hardy Vegetable Soup (KC)
59   Vegetable-Beef Soup (EB)
59   Cream of Mushroom Soup (CD)
60   Baked Potato Soup (MW)
61   Tortilla Soup (CD)
62   **SALADS**
62   Bride's Fruit Salad (CD)
62   Sauerkraut Slaw (EB)
63   Chicken Salad (CD)
63   Pea-Cheese Salad (CD)
64   Caesar Salad (KC)
64   Tossed Vegetable-Cheese Salad (LC)
65   Pineapple-Cheese Salad (CD)
65   24-Hour Slaw (EB)
66   Southwestern Tossed Salad (CD)
66   Potato Salad (EB)
66   Three-Bean Salad (EB)
67   **DRESSINGS & SAUCES**
67   Mayonnaise (CD)
67   Horseradish Sauce (CD)
68   Cilantro Dressing (CD)
68   Cooked Salad Dressing (CD)
68   Blue Cheese Dressing (CD)
69   Tangy French Dressing (KC)
69   Western Dressing (CD)
69   Whipped Onion-Garlic Butter (CD)
70   Western Vegetable Dip (CD)

x

OLD-FASHIONED RECIPES/TABLE OF CONTENTS

70   Cheese Dip (LC)
70   Crab Dip (LC)
71   Simple Mustard Dip (CD)
71   Cranberry Sauce (KC)
71   Cranberry Frappé (KC)
72   **VEGETABLE SIDE DISHES**
72   Asparagus Loaf (CD)
72   Carrot Fritters (EB)
73   Baked Beans (LC)
73   Creamed Carrots (EB)
73   Sweet Creamed Carrots (EB)
74   Quick Potato Casserole (CD)
74   Eggplant au Gratin (MW)
75   Asparagus with Sour Cream Sauce (MW)
75   Baked Cabbage (EB)
75   Creamed String Beans (CD)
76   French Style Green Peas (CD)
76   Corn Fritters (EB)
76   Fried Cucumbers (EB)
77   Fried Okra (EB)
77   Fried Eggplant (LC)
77   Cheese Carrots (LC)
78   Fried Tomatoes with Thyme and Garlic (MW)
78   Golden Onion Rings (LC)
79   Mashed Potatoes (EB)
79   New Potatoes (KC)
80   Stuffed Eggplant (KC)
80   Stuffed Mushrooms (MW)
81   Cheese Noodle Ring (KC)
81   Spanish Rice (CD)
82   Sweet Potatoes with Pineapple (CD)
82   Stuffed Onions (CD)
82   Turnip Greens and Hog Jowl (LS)
83   Baked Corn (EB)
83   Scalloped Tomatoes (CD)
84   **PICKLES & RELISHES**
84   Curtido/Carrot Relish (CD)
84   Dilly Cucumbers (EB)
85   Marinated Artichoke Hearts (CD)

85	Tomato Preserves (CD)
86	Bread and Butter Pickles (EB)
86	Easy Corn Relish (KC)
87	Hot Chow-Chow (CD)
88	Watermelon Rind Preserves (EB)
88	Dill Pickles (EB)
89	**JAMS & JELLIES**
89	Orange Marmalade (KC)
89	Jalapeno Pepper Jelly (CD)
90	Grape Jelly (CD)
90	Pineapple-Cherry Jam (KC)
90	Strawberry Jam (KC)
91	Blackberry Jam (EB)
91	Plum Jelly (KC)
91	Plum Marmalade (KC)
92	**BEVERAGES**
92	Sugar Syrup (CD)
92	Lemonade (CD)
92	Fruit Punch (KC)
93	Ching-a-ling Float (CD)
93	Tropical Cocktail (CD)
93	Cranberry Punch (CD)
94	Party Punch (LC)
94	Fruit Milk Shake (LC)
94	Pot of Tea (KC)
95	Iced Tea (KC)
95	Russian Tea (KC)
95	Hot Mulled Cider (LS)
96	Orange Julius (EB)
96	Hardy-Party Punch (LC)
97	**MEASUREMENTS & CONVERSIONS**
98	**THANK YOU**
98	**ORDERING INFORMATION**
99	**COMING ATTRACTION**

BISCUITS & BREADS

Buttermilk Biscuits
2 cups sifted flour
3 teaspoons baking powder
¾ teaspoon baking soda
¾ teaspoon salt
4 tablespoons softened butter or shortening
¾ cup buttermilk

Preheat oven to 425 degrees Fahrenheit (F). Sift flour once, then combine flour, baking soda, baking powder, and salt, sifting together into a large mixing bowl. Cut soft butter or shortening into dry ingredients with a fork or pastry cutter until mixture resembles coarse cornmeal. Add buttermilk slowly until dough is firm (amount needed may vary). Turn out on a lightly floured board and knead gently until surface of dough is smooth. Roll or pat out to ½-inch thickness. Dip biscuit cutter in flour then cut out biscuits and place on a lightly floured and greased baking sheet so that biscuits are touching each other. Brush top of biscuits with melted butter, and bake until golden brown (approximately 10 to 12 minutes) in 425 degree oven. Makes 18 biscuits.

Hints: (1) Baking powder and baking soda both loose their "zest" over time, especially in humid climates. If biscuits do not rise as expected, this could be the problem. The remedy is to check the expiration date and, if expired, buy fresh.

(2) Calibrate your oven temperature with your first batch of biscuits to determine appropriate baking temperature. At around eight minutes, check to see if the biscuits have reach the desired golden brown. If not, give them another couple of minutes and check again. If your oven cooks "too quickly," you should reduce recipe temperatures.

(3) There are those who say that a really good biscuits requires the use of lard rather than butter or a vegetable shortening. Use your own judgment.

(4) In a pinch, you can substitute one capful (approximately 1 teaspoon) of vinegar in fresh milk for buttermilk.

Biscuit Gravy

¼ cup bacon or sausage drippings or butter
2 to 4 tablespoons flour
salt and pepper to taste
½ cup milk
1 to 2 cups water (as needed)
1 piece bacon or one piece sausage crumbled

Place fresh bacon or sausage drippings (left over after frying bacon or sausage) or butter in a skillet over medium heat and add flour, salt, and pepper (okay to use leftover flour-mix from biscuits). Stir constantly until mixture bubbles, then add milk slowly and keep stirring. If too thick, add water until desired consistency for spooning gravy over biscuits. Crumble bacon or sausage into gravy and heat for about one minute more, then serve hot with biscuits.

Hint: For a brown gravy, spread the flour in the bottom of the skillet first and stir until it becomes an amber brown, then add bacon or sausage drippings and stir until the mixture bubbles.

Plain Biscuits

2 cups flour
3 teaspoons baking powder
¾ teaspoon salt
¾ cup milk
4 tablespoons soft butter or shortening

Preheat oven to 425 degrees F. Sift flour once then add baking powder and salt and sift all together into mixing bowl. Cut butter or shortening (with fork or pastry cutter) into dry ingredients until mixture resembles coarse cornmeal. Stir in milk slowly until dough is soft but sticky. Turn out on lightly floured board and knead until surface of dough is smooth. Roll or pat until ½-inch thick. Cut biscuits out with a lightly floured cutter and place on a lightly floured, greased baking sheet so that they are touching. Bake in hot (425 degree F) oven 10 to 15 minutes. Makes 1 to 1½ dozen biscuits. For a spoon-drop biscuit, increase amount of milk.

Biscuit Variations

Orange Biscuit: add one tablespoon grated orange rind and one teaspoon sugar to flour mixture.

Cheese Biscuit: add ½ cup grated cheddar cheese to batter.

Lunch Biscuit: add one teaspoon sugar to the dry ingredients.

Richer Biscuit: use 6 tablespoons shortening and reduce buttermilk.

Drop Biscuit: increase milk for a thinner batter.

Cornbread

2 cups flour
1 cup cornmeal
½ cup sugar
1 teaspoon salt
1½ teaspoons baking powder
2 eggs
1 cup milk
2 tablespoons butter or cooking oil

Preheat oven to 350 degrees F. Grease bread pan or skillet. Sift dry ingredients together. Add eggs, cooking oil, and milk to dry ingredients. Whisk or beat together until batter is smooth. Pour batter into preheated greased pan and bake until golden brown, usually 20 to 30 minutes. Serves six.

Buttermilk Cornbread

2 cups cornmeal
1 cup flour
½ teaspoon salt
½ teaspoon baking soda
1 teaspoon baking powder
2 eggs
3 tablespoons melted shortening
1 cup buttermilk

Preheat oven to 400 degrees F. Mix dry ingredients together, then add shortening and stir. Add eggs then buttermilk slowly and beat until batter is smooth. Pour into a well greased baking pan or skillet. Bake to golden brown, about 30 to 40 minutes. Serves six.

Pinches/Mexican Corn Muffins
To Basic Cornbread or Buttermilk Cornbread recipe, add:
1 cup (or can) whole kernel corn (drain well)
½ jalapeno pepper, seeded and finely chopped
½ cup cheddar cheese, shredded
2 tablespoons cilantro leaves, finely chopped

Prepare as for cornbread. **Hint:** wear rubber gloves when chopping jalapeno peppers and don't touch face or eyes.

Cornbread Variations
Use plain or buttermilk cornbread recipes

Cornbread Muffins: pour batter into muffin tins instead of skillet or bread pan.

Onion Cornbread: add one finely-chopped onion to batter.

Real Corn Cornbread: add one can drained whole kernel corn to batter.

Jalapeno Cornbread: add one seeded and finely chopped jalapeno pepper to batter. Can also include whole kernel corn (see Pinches recipe).

Cracklin' Cornbread: add one cup cracklings, finely chopped.

Hush Puppies, make Onion Cornbread and drop batter by small spoonfuls into hot (350 degrees F) fat and fry until golden brown.

Bran Muffins

1 cup bran
¾ cup flour
4 teaspoons baking powder
½ teaspoon salt
1 egg
2 tablespoons molasses
½ cup milk
½ cup raisins (optional)

Preheat oven to 375 degrees F. Grease muffin tin (can spray with cooking oil spray). Sift together flour, baking powder, and salt into a bowl. Add bran and mix well, then add beaten egg, molasses, milk, and raisins (optional). Beat well. Pour into muffin tin. Bake at 375 degrees for 20 minutes or golden brown.

Easy Nut Bread

3 cups sifted flour
4 teaspoons baking powder
1 teaspoon salt
1 cup sugar
1 egg, unbeaten
¼ cup melted shortening
1¼ cups milk
1 cup broken nut meats

Preheat oven to 350 degrees F. Melt shortening and cool. Grease 8- by 4-inches loaf pan or spray with cooking oil spray. Sift together flour, baking powder, salt, and sugar. Beat in melted shortening, egg, and milk until batter is creamy. Add nuts and stir. Pour into loaf pan and bake about one hour or until golden brown and firm to touch.

Waffles
2 cups flour
2 teaspoons baking powder
½ teaspoon salt
2 tablespoons cooking oil
2 eggs
1½ - 2 cups milk

Heat waffle iron or skillet on medium heat. Sift flour, baking powder, and salt together. Add cooking oil and eggs to flour. Mix well. Add milk, blending until batter is smooth and will pour easily. Add sufficient oil or butter to heated waffle iron or skillet to prevent sticking. Spoon or pour batter onto grill or skillet, being careful not to overload. Turn when surface of waffle bubbles and cook other side. Serves eight.

Variations
Add blueberries, strawberries, or other fruit to the batter.

Pop Overs
1 cup flour
½ teaspoon salt
2 eggs
1 tablespoon melted shortening
¾ cup milk

Preheat oven to 450 degrees F. Sift flour before measuring. Grease pop over pan or tall glass (oven proof) custard cups generously then preheat them. Melt shortening and cool. Sift together flour and salt. Add egg and cooled melted shortening, then milk, beating until batter is smooth. Fill hot pan or custard cups half full of batter. Bake for 20 minutes, then reduce heat to 350 degrees F and bake for 10 to 15 minutes longer or until golden brown. Makes ten to twelve pop overs.

Sweet Rolls or Coffee Cake

6 to 8 cups sifted flour
1 teaspoon salt
½ cup sugar
2 cakes yeast
¼ cup warm water
1¼ cups milk, scalded
¼ cup shortening
2 eggs, well beaten

Preheat oven to 375 degrees F. Soften yeast in warm water. Scald milk. Add shortening, sugar, and salt to milk. Cool to lukewarm, then blend in flour to make a thick batter. Add yeast mixture and eggs to batter and beat well. Add additional flour if needed to make a soft dough. Turn on lightly floured board and knead until satiny. Form into a ball, place in greased bowl, cover, and let rise until double in bulk. Punch down, shape into rolls or coffee cake or loaves. Let rise until double in size again. Bake in moderate (375 degree) oven for 25 to 30 minutes. Serves six to ten.

Sourdough Bread

Bread Starter:
1 package dry yeast
2 cups warm water
2 tablespoons sugar
2 cups flour

Dissolve yeast in warm water (use a stoneware crock or glass jar). Add sugar, then flour slowly, mixing well. Cover loosely and set in a warm place. Let ferment for 48 hours. Use a closed glass jar to store in refrigerator for future use. Can be kept in refrigerator for at least six months. When some is taken out, add like amount of flour and water to bring back to original consistency and amount. After replacing, let set at room temperature until mixture bubbles (about 4 hours), then place back in refrigerator.

Sourdough Bread

6½ cups flour
1 package dry yeast
3 tablespoons sugar
2 tablespoons salt
1 cup sourdough starter
1¼ cups warm water
¼ cup yellow cornmeal
1 to 2 tablespoons butter, melted

Place yeast in warm water to dissolve. Add starter and mix well. Then add 1½ cups flour, blending well. Cover and set in warm place and let ferment for at least 12 hours. Stir, add salt and sugar and mix well. Then slowly add 3½ cups flour, blending well. Place dough on floured board (with remaining flour) and knead flour into the dough. Knead for at least 10 minutes. Place into a greased bowl, cover, and let rise until doubled. Punch dough down, divide into two parts, and place on floured board again. Roll into loaf shape. Sprinkle cornmeal on greased baking sheet and place loaves on baking sheet. Cover, set aside, let rise until double in size again. Using a sharp knife, make slanted cuts on tops of loaves.

Preheat oven to 450 degrees F. Brush top of loaves with melted butter. Place loaves in oven along with a pan of water. Bake 35 to 40 minutes until loaves are a golden brown. **Variation: Sourdough Rolls** can be made by pinching batter into roll size pieces.

Sourdough Biscuits

½ cup sourdough starter
2 cups flour
2½ teaspoons baking powder
1 teaspoon salt
½ cup shortening
¾ cup milk

Preheat oven to 400 degrees F. Sift flour, baking powder and salt together. Cut shortening into flour mix until it makes a crumbly mixture. Stir in sourdough starter with just enough milk to make a dough. Knead gently, roll out, cut into biscuits, and place on greased pan. Bake for 10 to 12 minutes or until golden brown.

Variation: For Sourdough Cheese bread/rolls/biscuits, add one cup grated cheddar cheese to the mixture.

Potato Muffins

1 cup mashed potatoes
1 cup cornmeal
½ cup flour
3 teaspoons baking powder
1 teaspoon sugar (optional)
1 teaspoon salt
1 egg, beaten
2 tablespoons vegetable oil

Preheat oven to 350 degrees F. Sift together cornmeal, flour, baking powder, salt, and sugar. Combine beaten egg, oil, potatoes, and milk. Beat well then stir into dry ingredients, beating until batter is well mixed. Baked in greased muffin pan for 30 minutes. Makes approximately 1 dozen muffins.

MAIN COURSE
Chicken

Chicken and Dumplings
Stewed Chicken
1 large fryer
Sufficient water to fill large soup pot
Salt and pepper to taste
1 medium onion, diced
2 to 3 stalks celery, diced
2 to 3 medium carrots, diced

Cut chicken into parts, place in stew pan, add salt, pepper, onion, celery, carrot, and boil until tender (approximately 2 hours), adding water as needed. Once tender, remove chicken from broth. Cool chicken. Separate meat from bone and chop into small chunks. Return meat to broth, and bring to light boil.

Drop Dumplings
2 cups flour
3 teaspoons baking powder
1 teaspoon salt
2 tablespoons butter (room temperature)
1 egg
¾ cup milk

Sift together dry ingredients. Work in butter with your fingertips. Break egg into the center. Add milk gradually, stirring, to make a stiff batter. Drop by small spoonfuls on top of chicken and cook until done—fluffy dumplings done in center. Serves six to eight.

Southern Fried Chicken

1 large fryer, cut up
1 cup shortening
½ cup butter
1 cup flour in a large bowl
salt and pepper and poultry spices to taste
2 eggs, beaten

Melt shortening and butter in a frying pan. Cut fryer into pieces. Sift flour, salt, pepper, and spices together in a bowl. Roll each piece of chicken in flour/salt/pepper/spice mixture. Dip floured chicken in beaten eggs and roll into flour mixture again. Drop in boiling fat. Fry until golden brown. Drain on paper towel, then serve immediately. Serves six.

Fried Chicken Gravy

Pour most of the fat from the frying pan. Add 2 to 3 tablespoons of flour mixture left from coating chicken. Heat to bubbling. Add approximately one cup milk and additional water if needed to thin. Serve with fried chicken and biscuits.

Diet Chicken

1 chicken, roasted or baked
1 green bell pepper
1 white onion
1 can stewed tomatoes

Remove chicken from bone and chop into bite-size pieces. Chop pepper and onion into ½- to 1-inch size pieces. Lightly spray a skillet with cooking oil spray and sauté bell pepper and onion. Add chicken and tomatoes and stir, cooking an additional three to five minutes. Serves six.

Curry Chicken

Stewed or baked chicken
1½ cups cooked rice
¼ cup diced onion
1 tablespoon mayonnaise
½ teaspoon curry powder
2 teaspoons vinegar
6 to 8 celery sticks, chopped (1 cup)
1 green pepper, chopped (½ cup)
Pepper, dash
½ cup mayonnaise
Nuts (if desired)

Cook rice according to directions on package. Remove bone from chicken and chop into small pieces. Combine with all other ingredients except mayonnaise in a skillet or shallow pan and sauté. Take off heat, stir in mayonnaise and serve over rice. Serves eight.

Chicken-Green Bean Casserole

2 cups chicken (cut into ½- to 1-inch pieces)
2 cups whole green beans
2 cans cream of chicken soup
½ cup or less milk or broth
1 can water chestnuts
1 tablespoon mayonnaise
1 teaspoon curry powder
1 can French fried onion rings

Heat cream of chicken soup on medium heat. Add curry powder and mayonnaise. Butter casserole dish and line bottom with green beans. Pour some soup mix on beans. Add chicken layer. Continue to layer beans, soup mix, and chicken. Bake for 15 minutes at 350 degrees F, then add onion rings. Heat 10 minutes more to brown onion rings. Serves eight.

Chicken Baked in Wine

4 chicken breasts (skin removed)
4 tablespoons butter
½ teaspoon each sage, rosemary, and thyme
½ cup onion, chopped
2 cups white wine
½ to 1 pound mushrooms (sliced)
1 cup rice
¼ cup flour

Combine butter, onions, mushrooms, and seasoning in pan or skillet on medium heat and simmer until onions are clear. Add wine and cook for one minute. Place chicken in a skillet and cover with hot mixture, then cover skillet and cook on low to medium heat for approximately 30 minutes. Prepare rice according to directions on package. When chicken is done, remove from pan. Add flour to pan drippings to make sauce, adding water if needed. Serve chicken with sauce over rice. Serves four.

King Ranch Chicken

1 large fryer
1 large onion
1 large green pepper
1 package tortillas
1 can chicken stock or soup
½ pound cheddar cheese, grated
1½ teaspoons chili powder
garlic salt to taste
1 can condensed cream of mushroom soup
1 can tomatoes, crushed

Stew or bake chicken. Remove chicken from bone and cut in bite-size pieces. Chop onion and bell peppers into ½- to 1-inch chunks. In large, buttered casserole dish, combine prepared chicken, onion, and green pepper. Add a layer of tortilla strips which have been dipped into hot stock just long enough to soften. Layer with chicken, then onions and green peppers, then tortilla strips until all are used. Top off with grated cheese and sprinkle with chili powder and garlic salt. Then add in order, giving a little time to soak into layers, chicken stock or soup, mushroom soup, and tomatoes. Bake in moderate (350 degrees F) oven 30 to 45 minutes. Serves eight to ten.

Chicken Spaghetti
(Great recipe for large group)

2 fryers or 4 to 5 pounds chicken pieces
3 ribs celery, diced
1 green pepper, diced
2 onions, diced
2 cloves garlic, crushed
1 can (4 ounces) mushroom stems and pieces
1 package spaghetti, broken
1 large can tomatoes, chopped
2 tablespoons chopped ripe olives
1 can condensed cream of mushroom soup
1 teaspoon salt
¼ to ½ teaspoon pepper (to taste)
¼ teaspoon paprika
several dashes of Worcestershire sauce
1 pound Velveeta cheese, grated

Simmer chicken until tender in well-seasoned water. Remove chicken and broth. Measure one quart broth back into pan and add celery, green pepper, onions, garlic, and mushrooms. Cook for ten minutes over medium heat, then add spaghetti and cook until spaghetti is done. Add tomatoes, olives, soup, salt, pepper, and paprika. Bone and dice chicken. Add Worcestershire sauce and cheese to boned chicken, then add to spaghetti mixture and toss together. Serves twelve.

Chicken Parmesan
4 chicken breast or 8 thighs
½ cup grated Parmesan cheese
1 stick (¼ pound) butter, melted
1 package saltine crackers, crushed or
1 cup fine bread crumbs

Mix crushed crackers or crumbs and cheese. Dip chicken into butter, then roll in crumb mixture. Place in baking pan and bake at 325 degrees F for 1 hour. Serves four.

Chicken Salad Mold
4 to 5 pound stewing chicken
1 teaspoon salt
2 cups water
1 envelope unflavored gelatin
½ cup cold water
1 cup celery, diced
1 cup peas (small)
1 cup almonds, chopped, salted and blanched
5 hard-cooked eggs, chopped
1½ tablespoons lemon juice
1 cup mayonnaise

Cut chicken into large pieces and rub with salt. Place chicken in Dutch oven or large saucepan. Add water, cover, and simmer about 2 hours on medium heat or until tender. Add water during cooking so there is always 2 cups liquid in pan. Remove chicken. Keep broth hot. Cool chicken pieces. Remove skin and bone from chicken and discard. Chop meat finely. Soften gelatin in ½ cup water and add to the hot chicken broth and stir until dissolved. Stir in remaining ingredients, except mayonnaise. Cool. Fold in mayonnaise. Pour into a 12- x 8- x 2-inchs (or equivalent size) shallow dish. Chill until firm and cut into squares. Serve with additional mayonnaise. Yields 20 portions.

Other Poultry
Roast Duck
1 butcher prepared duck
Bread stuffing mixture:
8 to 10 slices toasted white bread, crumbled
1 onion, chopped
1 teaspoon salt (or to taste)
½ teaspoon pepper (or to taste)
1 egg, beaten
½ cup milk
¼ cup butter, melted

Combine bread stuffing ingredients (bread, onion, salt and pepper, egg, milk). Mix well. Stuff duck with mixture and sew up body cavity. Place in baking pan and baste with melted butter. Bake at 350 degrees F for about 1 hour, basting every 10 to 15 minutes with butter. Serves six.

Roast Quail
4 butcher prepared quail
bread stuffing mixture ingredients (see above)
4 fresh oysters

Combine same ingredients as for Roast Duck stuffing, except add one fresh oyster inside each bird. Stuff, bake at 350 degrees F for about 30 minutes or until done. Serves four.

Roast Turkey

12- to 20-pound turkey
2 teaspoons (or to taste) salt
1 teaspoon (or to taste) pepper
1 teaspoon (or to taste) poultry spices
¼ cup butter

If purchased frozen, thaw turkey by leaving in the refrigerator for 24 hours, then finish thawing in hot water in thoroughly cleaned kitchen sink just before cooking (and thoroughly clean sink afterwards as well as counter where bird was prepared). Remove all giblets from neck or chest cavity. Stuff bird, using one of the dressing recipes in this book, and truss cavity. Rub a mixture of salt, pepper, poultry spices, and butter on upper surface of turkey. Arrange turkey on a rack in a roasting pan. Roast at 350 degrees F, allowing 20 minutes cooking time for each pound of turkey. When done, cut and remove trussing threads, and place turkey, breast side up, on serving platter.

Oyster Stuffing

4 cups bread crumbs (day-old bread/toast)
1 tablespoons salt
½ cup melted butter or pan drippings
4 tablespoons parsley, diced
4 tablespoons lemon juice
½ teaspoon paprika
½ teaspoon poultry seasoning
1 large onion, diced
4 stalks celery, diced
1 cup finely chopped giblets
1 pint oysters
1 cup oyster liquor
½ to 1 cup milk
1 egg, beaten
(directions next page)

Remove neck and giblets packed in bird (keep digging, they'll be there). Place in a sauce pan with sufficient water to cover, adding salt, pepper, and poultry seasoning. Cook over medium heat until tender. Remove from heat, cool, remove flesh from neck (discard neck skin and bone) and remove and discard cover tissue of gizzard. Chop neck, liver, heart, and tender gizzard meat into ¼-inch or smaller pieces. Reserve ¼ cup of giblets for making gravy. Combine the remaining giblets with bread crumbs, salt, butter or pan drippings, parsley, onions, celery, giblets, lemon juice, and paprika. Add oysters (make sure all particles of shells have been removed), oyster liquor, egg, and milk. Mix well before stuffing turkey. Excess of what is needed to stuff bird can be baked in a casserole dish for the last 30 to 40 minutes of bird-cooking time. Serve with turkey and giblet gravy.

Giblet Gravy

½ cup turkey roasting pan drippings
¼ cup giblets, chopped finely
½ cup flour
salt and pepper to taste
½ to 1 cup milk

Stir flour, salt, and pepper into a skillet with pan drippings from roasted turkey and cook on medium heat until mixture bubbles. Add milk, stirring constantly until gravy is smooth. If additional thinning is needed, add water. When desired consistency is reached add giblets. Heat for another minute. Serve with turkey and dressing.

Mushroom Nut Stuffing

1 cup thinly sliced mushrooms
1 cup onions, diced
1 cup chopped walnuts
4 cups bread or cracker crumbs
1 teaspoon salt
½ teaspoon paprika
1 teaspoon celery salt
1 egg, beaten

Mix all ingredients together and stuff turkey. Bake excess in casserole dish for last 30 to 40 minutes of bird-cooking time. Serve with turkey and gravy.

Chestnut Stuffing

1 quart chestnuts
1 cup soft bread crumbs
½ cup butter/shortening, melted
1 onion, diced
2 stalks celery, diced
½ teaspoon salt
¼ teaspoon paprika
½ cup milk
1 egg, beaten

Boil chestnuts until tender. Remove shells and skins and mash through a sieve. Add all other ingredients and mix well before stuffing turkey. Bake excess in casserole dish for last 30 to 40 minutes of bird-cooking time. Serve with turkey and gravy.

Note: Chestnuts are an acquired taste. If you're not sure your guest love chestnut stuffing, then make one of the other stuffing recipes as well and serve the stuffings as a side dish.

Seafood

Gumbo

3 cups crab meat and/or shrimp, cleaned, cooked, chopped
1 teaspoon salt
¼ teaspoon black pepper
1 teaspoon chili powder
3 onions, diced
½ pound sliced bacon
1 cup rice (uncooked)
1 can tomatoes
2 cans tomato sauce
1 can okra (or 1 pound bag of frozen okra)
1 quart water

Prepare uncooked rice according to directions on the package. Cut bacon into small pieces and fry in skillet. Add onions, salt, pepper, and chili powder to skillet. Stir, then scrape all into a large stock kettle. Add okra, tomatoes, tomato sauce, and one quart water. Cook slowly over medium heat for 30 minutes. Add crab or shrimp (or both) and cook another 10 minutes. Serve over rice. Serves eight.

Creamed Tuna

1 can water-packed tuna
2 tablespoons butter
2 tablespoons flour
½ cup milk
1 small dill pickle, diced
¼ cup lemon juice

Melt butter in skillet over medium heat, add flour, then milk and water packed with tuna. Cook until thickened. Add diced pickle and lemon juice, then flaked tuna from can. Salt and pepper to taste. Serve hot on toast.

Salmon Croquettes

1 pound salmon, bone removed, finely chopped
1 cup cream
1 egg beaten
3 tablespoons flour
1 tablespoon butter
1 teaspoon salt
1 tablespoon parsley, minced
dash cayenne pepper
2 tablespoons lemon juice
bread crumbs

Combine salmon, salt, parsley, cayenne and lemon juice in mixing bowl. Cut butter into flour. Place cream in a saucepan and bring to a boil then stir flour/butter mix into the boiling cream. Cook for 2 minutes. Sir in salmon mixture, combining all ingredients. Let cool. Form into croquettes and roll first in beaten eggs, then bread crumbs. Fry in hot oil. Serves six.

Flaked Fish Casserole

2 cups perch, cooked, flaked
(can substitute crabmeat, salmon or lobster for perch)
½ cup grated Cheddar cheese
2 eggs
2 cups milk
3 crackers, rolled into crumbs
2 tablespoons butter, melted
juice of 1 lemon

Combine fish flakes and cheese, add beaten eggs and milk, and pour into buttered casserole. Cover with cracker crumbs and melted butter. Pour lemon juice over all. Cover and set casserole dish in pan of warm water in oven. Bake at 350 degrees F for 30 minutes. Serves six.

Scalloped Oysters

1 to 2 dozen oysters, shelled
(if bought shelled in container, save oyster juice)
2 cups cracker crumbs
1 cup butter, melted
4 tablespoons cream
salt and pepper to taste

Mix butter and cracker crumbs. Line bottom of a casserole dish with a layer of crumbs mixture, then add a layer of oysters. Continue layering with crumbs and oysters until all are used. Sprinkle with salt and pepper. Dribble cream and oyster juice over mixture. Bake at 350 degrees F for 45 minutes and serve hot. Serves six.

Fish Fritters

1 pound fish fillets
3 eggs, separated
3 tablespoons flour
1 teaspoon minced garlic
1 teaspoon minced parsley
1 teaspoon salt
¼ teaspoon pepper

Broil or boil fish, remove bone, flake, then mash. Beat egg yolks. Add flour slowly to egg yolks, then garlic, parsley, salt and pepper, mixing as you add each ingredient. Stir in fish. Beat egg whites until frothy and blend into fish mixture. Drop from spoon into hot oil and fry to a golden brown. Drain fritters on paper towels. Serves four.

Meats
Meat Loaf

1 pound ground beef or veal
½ pound ground pork
2 stalks celery
1 medium onion
1 medium green pepper
1 cup bread crumbs
(or ½ cup crumbs and ½ cup dry oatmeal)
1 egg, beaten
¾ cup milk
1 teaspoon salt
½ teaspoon black pepper
¼ teaspoon red pepper
¼ cup tomato sauce or catsup (optional)

Clean and dice celery, onion, and green pepper Mix all ingredients together and form into a loaf. Bake at 375 degrees F for one to 1½ hour. Serves six.

Stuffed Green Peppers

1 pound ground meat
1 large onion, diced
2 to 4 celery stalks, diced
1 can tomatoes
6 to 8 green peppers

Dice onions and celery and fry together with ground meat. Remove excess fat. Add one can tomatoes and cook until mushy. Fill cored and seeded green peppers with mixture. Top with shredded cheese. Bake with a little water in bottom of pan at 350 degrees F for 45 minutes. Serves six to eight. For an alternate recipe, stuff peppers with meat loaf mixture (see recipe for meat loaf) and bake.

Roast Beef

2- to 4-pound roast
(round or standing rib with ribs removed)
salt and pepper to taste
½ teaspoon cinnamon
1 clove garlic, segmented

Sprinkle salt, pepper, and cinnamon over surfaces of roast and place roast in an open pan or large skillet. Insert peeled garlic segments into slits in roast. Place in a 500 degree F oven and sear for 20 to 30 minutes or until lightly browned. Reduce temperature to 300 degrees F and continue roasting until beef is cooked according to taste: allow 16 minutes cooking time per pound for a rare roast, 22 minutes per pound for a medium roast, and 30 minutes per pound for a well done roast. After temperature has been reduced, vegetables can be added to pan/skillet. Potatoes, carrots, celery stalks, and onions cut into chunks are a good choice. Vegetables will be more juicy if pan is covered with foil for continued cooking. Serves six to eight.

Sausage and Onion Casserole

1 pound sausage
1 can mushrooms, drained
1 can cream of chicken soup
2 cups grated cheddar cheese
1 large onion, diced
2 cans French fried onion rings
rice or noodles, prepared according to package directions

Cook sausage over low heat until brown. Add onion and cook 5 minutes longer. Drain grease from pan. Add soup and other ingredients, then simmer 10 to 15 minutes. Serve over rice or noodles cooked to directions on package. Top with French fried onion rings. Serves six to eight.

Chili

2 pounds beef round
6 dried red chili peppers
¼ cup cooking oil
3 buttons garlic
3 onions
2 tablespoons salt
1 teaspoon black pepper
2 cups water
1 tablespoon flour (for thickening)
½ cup water (for thickening)

Dice garlic and onions. Cut beef into ½- to 1-inch cubes. Sear beef in a skillet on high heat and remove from heat. Use oil in pan only if beef is very lean and skim off any excess oil after browning. Seed red peppers and boil in water 20 minutes. Remove skin, mash, add to skillet with beef, and brown on medium heat. Add the water that peppers were boiled in, onion, garlic, salt and black pepper, and more water if needed to cover meat. Cook about four hours. Thicken with 1 tablespoon flour (dissolve in ½ cup water).

Chili with Beans

1 to 2 cups chili
1 to 1½ pounds dried navy beans
5 to 6 cups water
1 tablespoon salt

Prepare chili by the recipe above (it can be made ahead of time or while beans are cooking). Rinse beans to clean and remove any broken or distorted beans. Soak in water 6 to 8 hours (overnight). Drain beans and add beans to 5 to 6 cups fresh water in large soup kettle. Add salt. Bring to boil, then reduce heat and simmer 2 to 4 hours or until beans are tender. Mix cooked beans with chili. Serves ten to twelve.

Pork Chops with Apple Stuffing

6 thick-cut pork chops
2 tablespoons butter
¼ cup celery, diced
¼ cup onion, diced
3 tart apples, diced
¼ cup sugar
½ cup bread or cracker crumbs
salt and pepper to taste

Have butcher cut 1- to 1½-inch thick pork chops and slice a pocket cut in the middle of each chop. Sauté celery, onions, and apples in butter. Sprinkle with sugar, cover, and cook slowly over medium heat (about 10 minutes) until tender and glazed. Add bread crumbs and dash of salt and pepper. Stuff chop pockets with mixture. Place in baking pan, add a few tablespoons water, cover, and cook about one hour. Serves six.

Barbecued Ribs

3 pounds ribs (beef or pork)
salt and pepper to taste
½ cup brown sugar
½ cup catsup
¼ cup mustard

Combine brown sugar, catsup, and mustard into a barbecue sauce. Cut ribs into serving size pieces, sprinkle with salt and pepper, and brown in skillet. Spread sauce over top and bake (covered) in 350 degree F oven for 2 hours.

Sweet and Sour Pork Chops

6 lean pork chops, trimmed of all fat
1 can (8 oz.) pineapple chunks packed in juice
¼ cup all-purpose flour
½ teaspoon salt
¼ teaspoon pepper
1 teaspoon cooking oil
½ cup cider vinegar
¼ cup firmly packed brown sugar
3 tablespoons sugar
1 tablespoon Worcestershire sauce
1 cup carrots, coarsely shredded
¼ cup green onions, chopped

Combine flour, salt, and pepper in plastic bag. Add pork chops and shake to coat. Brown flour-coated chops in oil in large skillet over medium heat. Pour off excess fat. Drain pineapple, saving juice. Combine juice, vinegar, brown sugar, white sugar, Worcestershire sauce, and the flour remaining in bag. Pour over chops and simmer over low heat, covered, for 30 minutes. Add pineapple, carrots, and green onions. Cover and simmer for another 15 to 20 minutes or until pork chops are tender. Prepare rice according to recipe on package. Serve pork chops with rice. Serves six.

Liver and Onions

1 pound calves liver
½ cup flour
salt and pepper to taste
1 large onion, sliced
2 tablespoons cooking oil

Slice liver into approximately 3-inch pieces. Add salt and pepper to flour and cooking oil to skillet. Dredge liver pieces in flour mix and fry, browning both sides of liver. Add onion slices and continue cooking until tender. Serves four to six.

DESSERTS
Cakes

I visited my Grandma on the family farm almost daily when I was a little girl since her house was just a mile walk from my elementary school. Grandma always let me help her (the best play for a child) gather eggs from the hen house, churn butter on the back porch, or that most wonderful thing—bake a cake. She sifted the flour three to four times before she measured it for the bowl, then folded the other ingredients in at just at the right time, using farm-fresh eggs and butter and only cake flour. Best of all, I got to lick the spoon and bowl and wait patiently for the cake to emerge from the oven so I could frost it. Then I got to lick the icing bowl and spoon, too. So, if you've gather eggs from the hen-house and have churn-fresh butter close by, here's what you need to do to make the tastiest cakes on the planet.

Grandma's Cake-Making Instructions

1. Sift flour twice before measuring, then once after.

2. All measurements are level with the mark, not heaping.

3. Eggs and milk should be at room temperature.

4. Add sugar to the butter or shortening slowly and beat well until the mixture is creamy. Then add eggs and beat until the sugar, shortening and eggs mixture is light and fluffy. If a liquid flavoring is used (such as vanilla), add it to this mixture.

5. Alternate adding sugar/shortening mixture and liquids to flour mixture, beginning and ending with flour mixture and blending well after each addition.

6. Use the right pan size. If the recipe calls for two 9-inch round pans, use two 9-inch round pans.

Grandma's Yellow Cake

2½ cups cake flour (preferred) or all-purpose flour
2 teaspoons baking powder
1 teaspoon salt
½ cup butter
3 brown eggs, unbeaten
1½ cups sugar
1½ teaspoons vanilla
1 cup milk

Preheat oven to 375 degrees F. Prepare two 9-inch cake pans by greasing pan bottom and sides (you can use a spray cooking oil), then lining bottom with wax paper cut to an exact fit and dusting wax paper with flour. In a large mixing bowl, cream butter and sugar until thoroughly blended. Add eggs, one at a time, beating well. Add vanilla to mixture and blend well. Sift flour, baking powder, and salt together twice. Add dry ingredients then milk a little at a time, mixing thoroughly before additional amounts are added. Pour equal portions of batter into prepared cake pans. Bake in 375 degree F oven for 25 to 30 minutes. Do not open oven for at least 20 minutes into baking or cake will fall. At 25 minutes, test cake by sticking wooden toothpick into center. If it comes out clean, cake is done. When done, remove cake from oven, tap pan to separate cake from pan (you may need to run a knife around edge of pan). Slide cake out of pan and onto a cooling rack. Let cool at least 20 minutes before icing. Remove wax paper from bottom of layers. Top cake with icing/frosting of your choice.

Variations of Grandma's Yellow Cake include:

Spice Cake
Grandma's Yellow Cake ingredients
1 teaspoon cinnamon (powdered)
¼ teaspoon nutmeg (powdered)
¼ teaspoon cloves (powdered)

Sift powdered spices with flour. Omit the vanilla from Grandma's Yellow cake recipe. Otherwise follow same procedure for mixing and baking cake.

Nut Cake
Grandma's Yellow Cake ingredients
½ cup chopped walnuts or pecans
Stir nuts into batter before placing in pan.

Fudge Cake
Grandma's Yellow Cake ingredients
3 squares melted chocolate
1 cup milk

Beat melted (but not hot) chocolate into sugar-egg mixture of yellow cake recipe. Beat thoroughly, then add the dry ingredients for yellow cake and milk as before.

Banana Cake
Grandma's Yellow Cake ingredients
6 ripe bananas, mashed
½ cup sour cream

Mash bananas in ½ cup of the 1½ cups sugar of the Yellow Cake recipe. Blend in sour cream, then combine with other ingredients according to Yellow Cake recipe.

Grandma's Devil's Food Cake

2½ cups cake flour
2 tablespoons baking powder
½ teaspoon baking soda
1 teaspoon salt
½ cup butter or shortening
1 cup white sugar
1 cup light brown sugar
2 eggs
1 cup milk
1 teaspoon vanilla
3 squares chocolate
¼ to ½ cup water

Preheat oven to 350 degrees F. Cream shortening and white and brown sugar together until light and fluffy. Add eggs, one at a time and beat well. Add vanilla to mixture and blend well. In a double boiler, combine chocolate and water over a low heat. Stir until thick and smooth, then cool slightly. Add chocolate to first mixture and blend well. Sift dry ingredients together twice, then alternate adding chocolate mixture and milk to the flour mixture, beating well after each addition. When batter is smooth and creamy, pour into two 9-inch well-greased pans (can use spray cooking oil) lined with wax paper. Bake in 350 degree oven for 30 to 35 minutes. Cool on rack and remove wax paper from bottom of layers. Place one layer on cake plate. Spread "Fluffy Icing" (see recipe this book) on first layer. Place second layer on top of first, then frost top and sides of cake. Garnish with chopped nuts or chocolate chips.

Gingerbread

1½ cups flour
1 teaspoon soda
½ teaspoon salt
1 teaspoon ginger
1 teaspoon cinnamon
½ cup sugar
3 tablespoons butter
1 egg
½ cup milk
½ cup molasses
cooking oil spray

Preheat oven to 350 degrees F. Sift dry ingredients together. Cut butter into sugar and blend until creamy. Add beaten egg and blend well. Mix milk and molasses. Add mixtures of milk and molasses and sugar and butter to dry ingredients, stirring well until batter is smooth. Spray a 9- by 5-inch loaf pan with cooking oil spray, pour in batter, and bake at 350 degrees for 30 to 45 minutes.

Apricot-Nut Bread

2½ cups all-purpose flour
1 tablespoon baking powder
1 teaspoon salt
1 cup sugar
whites from 2 large egg, lightly beaten
½ cup milk
4 teaspoons grated orange rind
1 cup fresh orange juice
3 tablespoons applesauce
1 cup dried apricots, finely chopped
½ cup walnuts, finely chopped
cooking oil spray
(directions on next page)

Preheat oven to 350 degrees F. Sift dry ingredients together in a large mixing bowl. Combine milk and beaten eggs, make a well in center of mixture, and blend in milk and eggs. Combine orange rind, juice, and applesauce. Add to flour mixture, stirring until moist. Stir in apricots and walnuts, then pour batter into 9- by 5-inch loaf pan coated with cooking oil spray. Bake at 350 degrees F for one hour or until a wooden toothpick inserted in center comes out clean. Remove from pan. Let cool on a wire rack then serve.

Icings

The next challenge for the cake-baking cook is making an icing of the right consistency. My solution is to go to the grocery store and buy one of those little cans that will be the perfect consistency, even if lacking in taste. However, for those of you intent on making your own, here are Grandma's Icing recipes. Good luck!

Fluffy Boiled Icing

1 cup sugar
1 egg white
½ teaspoon flavoring (vanilla or other)
¼ teaspoons cream of tartar
3 tablespoons hot water

Combine egg white, sugar, cream of tartar, flavoring, and water in top of double boiler, beating until thoroughly mixed. Place over boiling water and beat constantly until icing stands in peaks. Remove from heat and add flavoring. Frost cake. Start by adding a layer of frosting to top of bottom layer. Place top layer over bottom. Frost sides, then top.

Fluffy Chocolate Icing

Follow recipe for Fluffy Boiled Icing. Melt 2 chocolate squares in a double boiler. When Fluffy Boiled Icing is done, remove from range and fold in chocolate. Do not beat after adding chocolate.

Chocolate Topping

2 tablespoons milk
2 tablespoons sugar
1 square sweet chocolate
1 square bitter chocolate

Mix milk and sugar together and bring to a boil. Shave sweet and bitter chocolate and stir until blended into the hot milk and sugar mixture. Cool. Spread on top of cake.

Creamy Butter Icing

4 tablespoons butter
2 cups confectioners' sugar
1/8 teaspoon salt
2 tablespoons cream or milk
1 teaspoon vanilla flavoring

Combine butter and one cup sugar, beating until light and creamy. Stir in remaining sugar, adding a little cream or milk from time to time as icing thickens. Add vanilla and salt and beat thoroughly. Makes sufficient icing to cover the tops of two 9-inch layers and sides of cake.

Chocolate Icing

3 tablespoons shortening
3 squares chocolate
1½ to 2 cups confectioner's sugar
¼ teaspoon salt
½ teaspoon vanilla
3 tablespoons hot milk

Mix shortening and chocolate together. Pour hot milk over sugar until dissolved, then add vanilla and salt. Add to chocolate mixture and beat until smooth and thick enough to spread. Covers two 9-inch layers and sides of cake.

Tarts & Patties

For tarts and patties, think miniature pies. Tarts generally contain a fruit or sweet mixture and patties contain a meat or a meat and vegetable mixture. For either, start with the standard pie pastry recipe and instead of 9-inch rounds, make smaller—muffin-pan size to 5-inch—rounds. Fill with the pie mixture of your choice and add a top crust. Alternatively, spoon filling onto ½ of pastry, fold over, and pinch together to make a package for the filling. Punch a few holes into top with a fork, then bake in a medium-heat (325 to 350 degrees F) oven for 20 to 25 minutes.

Pies

There are two ways to have a good pie crust. One is to buy one of those packages with two frozen crusts all ready for your pie filling. The other is to start from scratch the way your grandmother did. That way is paved with tears. For those of you determined to travel that road, Grandma's pie crust instructions might save your crust.

Grandma's Pie Crust Instructions

1. Shortening should reach room temperature before blending into flour, but water should be cold.

2. Use pastry flour and sift flour at least twice before blending in shortening.

3. Blend shortening into flour so that the mixture is like a coarse cornmeal, adding only enough liquid to dampen it. Too much moisture makes the crust tough, too little causes the pastry to crack while baking. Use the exact amount. Sprinkle cold water over flour mixture and toss lightly with a fork to dampen pastry.

4. Mold pastry into a round ball and place on a floured board. Roll lightly from center outward so that pie crust is roughly the shape of the pan and about 1/8-inch thick. Lower crust should be about 1-inch larger than pie pan. Move crust from board to pan by folding into quarters then unfolding into pan. Handling pastry too much or using too much flour makes for a tough crust. Be careful not to stretch dough when unfolding.

5. Grease pie pan with shortening, dust lightly, then fit pastry carefully into the pan so there is no air space between pastry and pan. Allow pastry to extend 1-inch over the edge. Fold overhang under to make an upright rim and flute edge by pinching crust between thumb and forefinger.

6. For two-crust pies, moisten the edge of the lower crust with water before placing the top crust onto the pie. Slash upper crust in several places to allow space for pie mixture to bubble. Brush crust with milk, cream, or butter before placing in preheated oven so it will brown evenly.

Plain Pie Pastry
(One Covered Pie or Two Open Pies)
2 cups flour
1 teaspoon salt
½ cup shortening
4 to 6 tablespoons cold water

Grease (okay to spray with cooking oil spray) pie pan(s). Let all ingredients except water set at room temperature for 20 minutes. Sift flour and salt together. Cut shortening into flour mix using pastry blender, knife, or finger tips. Stir in just enough cold water to dampen mixture. Dredge pastry board with flour. Using both hands, gather the mixture into a ball. Divide pastry, allowing more for lower crust than for upper crust. Dust with flour and roll ball of pastry lightly, from center to edge, keeping pastry as near the shape of pan as possible. Pick up pastry to move to pan by folding into quarters or rolling onto rolling pin, then unfold or unroll into pan. Fit pastry to pan. If a one-crust pie, fold overhang under to make an upright rim and flute the edge by pinching crust between thumb and forefinger. The recipe makes enough pastry for one covered pie or two open pies. Large quantities for more pies can be make by multiplying quantities of ingredients by number of pies desired. Unused pastry can be stored in a covered dish or plastic zip-lock bag in the refrigerator for up to one week. For a "rich" pastry, substitute ¼ cup cream cheese for an equal amount of shortening. Bake according to pie recipe.

Buttermilk Pie

½ cup flour
3½ cups sugar
1 teapoon salt
2 sticks oleo or butter, softened
6 whole eggs
1 cup buttermilk
2 tablespoons vanilla

Preheat oven to 350 degrees F. Combine sugar with softened butter, then blend in flour. Beat eggs slightly, then blend in buttermilk, salt, and vanilla. Add egg/buttermilk mixture to flour/sugar/butter mixture. Beat until batter is smooth. Pour into unbaked crust and bake at 350 degrees about 40 minutes. Makes two pies.

Pecan Pie

1 cup shelled pecans, chopped
12 to 24 pecan halves
1 cup corn syrup
2 eggs
½ cup sugar
1 tablespoon butter
1 teaspoon vanilla

Preheat oven to 375 degrees F. Combine all ingredients except the pecans and blend well. Mix in chopped pecans. Pour into unbaked pie crust. Add pecan halves to top. Bake at 375 degrees F for 15 minutes, then at 350 degrees for 30 minutes.

Apple Pie

6 to 8 large, tart apples
1 cup sugar
1 teaspoon cinnamon
¼ teaspoon nutmeg
¼ teaspoon salt
3 tablespoons flour
2 tablespoons butter

Preheat oven to 425 degrees F. Peel, core, and slice apples. Sift dry ingredients together. Line greased or oiled pie pan with pastry, allowing pastry to extend ½-inch over the plate. Fill with sliced apples. Sprinkle dry ingredients mixture over apples and dot with butter. Add top crust, extending crust ½-inch over edge of plate. Moisten the edge between crusts, then pinch together with a raised edge to form a pocket to hold in juices. Flute edge. Slash top crust to allow steam to escape and brush top with milk or cream. Bake at 425 degrees for 10 to 15 minutes or until edges begin to brown. Reduce temperature to 350 degrees F and bake 40 minutes longer.

Meringue:

Beat 3 egg whites with 3 teaspoons cold water. Add a few grains of salt or ¼ teaspoon cream of tartar. Beat until foamy (stiff peaks), adding 4 to 6 tablespoons sugar gradually.

Hint: To whip eggs well, they must be very fresh, with not a speck of egg yolk or grease. If sugar is added, add gradually after whites are beaten to the foamy stage and continue beating at medium mixer speed until whites stand in peaks. If beating with a whisk, use a cooper bowl. Do not use an aluminum bowl (discolors egg whites). Where recipes call for the meringue-topped pie to be returned to the oven until golden brown, check on meringue at three minutes and check again at four to make sure it does not burn. To avoid weepy meringue, spread to edge of pie all around.

Lemon Meringue Pie

1½ cups water
5 tablespoons cornstarch
4 tablespoons flour
½ teaspoon salt
2¼ cups boiling water
½ cup lemon juice
rind of 1 lemon, grated
3 eggs, separated into yolks and whites

Mix sugar, flour, cornstarch, and salt. Add boiling water, stirring constantly, until mixture thickens, then cook over low heat 10 minutes. Beat egg yolks slightly. Pour cornstarch mixture over eggs slowly, stirring constantly. Return to low heat and cook 2 minutes longer. Remove from heat, add lemon juice and grated rind. Cool mixture, pour into baked pie shell, cover with meringue and return to oven to brown.

Key Lime Pie

2 limes (or 4 key limes, which are smaller)
4 eggs, separated into yolks and whites
1 cup sugar
3 ounces lime gelatin
1 cup water
dash green food coloring (optional)
1 cup whipping cream
¼ teaspoon cream of tartar

Preheat oven to 375 degrees F and pre-bake pie crust. Scrape zest (green outer rind) then extract juice from limes. Combine egg yolks, ½ cup sugar, water, gelatin, a drop of green food coloring, zest of lime, and juice. Mix well and cook on low heat until thickened. Remove from heat and set pan in ice water, stirring until mixture is cooled and thickened. Whip cream and fold into mixture. Pour mixture into pre-baked pie crust and chill. Top with meringue (use ½ cup sugar, cream of tartar, egg whites) and brown.

Custard Pie

4 eggs, slightly beaten
6 tablespoons sugar
2½ cups milk
¼ teaspoon nutmeg or cinnamon
extra nutmeg or cinnamon to sprinkle over top of pie
1 teaspoon vanilla
¼ teaspoon salt

Preheat oven to 425 degrees F. Combine milk, sugar, salt, and flavoring, then add mixture to slightly beaten eggs. Blend until smooth. Line pie plate with pastry and build a fluted rim. Brush crust with melted butter or shortening. Pour in custard mixture and sprinkle with nutmeg or cinnamon. Bake at 425 degrees for 10 minutes. Reduce temperature to 350 degrees and bake 40 to 45 minutes or until custard is firm. Top with whipped cream.

Hint: When whipping cream, bowl and beater should be cold. Use a deep bowl with straight sides and whip with electric mixer (low speed) or wire whisk until thick and fluffy. Cream should double in volume. For topping, fold in a little sugar and vanilla.

Coconut Custard Pie

Add ½ cup shredded coconut to custard pie mixture before pouring into shell. Remove from oven at about 30 to 35 minutes and add shredded coconut to top as garnish. Finish baking another 5 to 10 minutes.

Sweet Potato Pie

2 cups sweet potatoes
3 eggs, separate yolks and whites
1 cup sugar
1 cup milk
2 teaspoons cinnamon
3 tablespoons sugar
¼ teaspoon cream of tartar

Bake sweet potatoes, remove peel, and mash. In a large mixing bowl, combine sweet potatoes, sugar, milk, cinnamon, and slightly beaten egg yolks. Blend until smooth. Pour into pie crust and bake at 375 degrees F for 40 to 45 minutes. Top with meringue and place under oven broiler for 2 to 4 minutes.

Pumpkin Pie

1½ cups pumpkin, canned or freshly cooked, mashed
½ cup sugar
2 cups milk
2 eggs, beaten
1 teaspoon each cinnamon, ginger, and salt

Preheat oven to 425 degrees F. Mix together pumpkin, sugar, milk, beaten eggs, spices, and salt. Blend well. Pour into unbaked pie crust. Bake at 450 degrees for 10 minutes, then reduce heat to 325 degrees and continue baking for another 20 to 30 minutes. Top with meringue and bake an additional 2 to 4 minutes or until golden brown. Or you can top with whipped cream when served.

Blackberry Pie

4 cups blackberries
1½ cups sugar
¼ teaspoon salt
2 tablespoons flour
1½ tablespoons butter
unbaked pie crust (bottom and top)

Preheat oven to 425 degrees F. Combine blackberries, sugar, salt, and flour. Pour mixture into a pie crust and spot butter around top. Cut pie crust top into strips and lattice to make a top crust. Bake at 425 degrees for 10 minutes, then reduce heat to 350 degrees and bake until crust is brown.

Hint: to prevent juice from running out of berry pies, make a paste of flour and water and spread paste around the edge of the bottom crust before adding top crust.

Blueberry Pie

4 cups blueberries
1 cup sugar
½ cup flour
½ teaspoon cinnamon
¼ teaspoon salt
1 tablespoon lemon juice
1½ tablespoons butter
unbaked pie crust (bottom and top)

Preheat oven to 425 degrees F. Line greased or oiled baking dish with an unbaked pie crust. Combine all ingredients, except butter, and mix well. Pour into pie crust and spot top with butter. Cut top crust into strips and lattice pastry. Bake at 425 degrees for 45 minutes or until crust is brown.

Rhubarb Pie

4 cups rhubarb
1¼ cups sugar
¼ cup orange juice
1 grated orange rind
5 tablespoons butter, separated
¼ teaspoon salt
2 tablespoons flour
unbaked pie crust (bottom and top)

Preheat oven to 425 degrees F. Line greased or oiled pie plate with bottom crust. Clean and chop rhubarb into ½-inch pieces. Combine rhubarb, sugar, flour, and salt and mix well. Blend in orange juice and rind. Pour into pie crust and spot with butter. Slice pie crust top into strips and lattice pastry on top. Bake at 425 degrees for about 20 minutes. Reduce heat to 350 degrees and bake for another 20 minutes.

Green Tomato Pie

4 to 5 green tomatoes, sliced
½ cup flour, sifted
1 cup sugar
¼ teaspoon salt
1 tablespoon butter
2 tablespoons vinegar
1½ teaspoons lemon extract
unbaked pie crust (bottom and top)

Preheat oven to 425 degrees F. Line oiled pie plate with bottom crust and cut top pie crust into strips. Mix lemon extract and vinegar together and soak sliced tomatoes in mixture for 20 minutes. Sprinkle bottom of pie crusts with ½ cup sugar. Dredge tomato slices in flour, then place in pie crust. Sprinkle salt and remaining flour over top and dot with butter. Sprinkle remaining sugar over tomatoes. Lattice top of pie. Bake at 425 degrees 30 minutes.

Cookies

Cookies come in four basic types: rolled, drop, bar, and refrigerator. For drop cookies, batter is dropped off the tip of a spoon. For best results use no more than one teaspoon of batter for each cookie and make sure there is adequate space (2-inch diameter around the drop) on the cookie sheet for the batter to spread. If the batter spreads into an adjacent cookie, you'll have little cakes instead of cookies.

Sugar Cookies

5 cups flour
1 teaspoons baking powder
1 teaspoon baking soda
1 teaspoon salt
2½ cups sugar
1 cup butter or shortening
1 teaspoon vanilla
1 cup milk
1 egg (optional)

Preheat oven to 375 degrees F. Sift together flour, baking powder, baking soda, and salt. Cut butter into sugar and blend until creamy. Add vanilla to sugar/butter mixture. If an egg is desired, beat it lightly and fold into sugar/butter mixture. Combine the sugar/butter mixture with the flour, adding milk and mixing well. Drop from tip of teaspoon onto greased baking sheets. Let stand a few minutes, then flatten cookies by stamping with a glass covered with a damp cloth. Sprinkle with sugar. Bake for 12 to 15 minutes at 375 degrees. Makes 8 dozen small cookies.

Hint: If you don't need 8 dozen sugar cookies, either reduce the quantity or split dry ingredients before adding wet ingredients and use splits to make peanut butter or oatmeal cookies. Other flavorings (maple, orange, etc.) can be added to the basic sugar cookie recipes as well.

Peanut Butter Cookies

Add 4 tablespoons crunchy peanut butter and ½ cup brown sugar to butter/egg/sugar mixture in the sugar cookie recipe.

Old-Fashioned Oatmeal Cookies

2 cups sifted flour
1 teaspoon baking soda
½ teaspoon salt
2 teaspoons cinnamon
2 cups quick-cooking oatmeal
1 cup brown sugar, firmly packed
1 cup granulated sugar
¾ cup shortening (soft)
2 eggs, beaten
½ cup milk (sour milk okay)
1 teaspoon vanilla
1 cup seeded raisins or chopped dates
½ cup nut meats, chopped

Let all ingredients reach room temperature. Grease cookie sheet and preheat oven to 375 degrees F. Sift together flour, baking soda, salt, cinnamon. Stir oatmeal into other dry ingredients. Blend brown sugar and granulated sugar into shortening. Beat eggs lightly, add vanilla, and blend into sugar/shortening, then blend all into flour mixture, adding milk until all is mixed together. Scrape bowl while beating. Add raisins and/or dates and chopped nuts. Drop from teaspoon on prepared cookie sheet. Bake at 375 degrees for 12 to 15 minutes. Makes up to 8 dozen cookies.

Orange Oatmeal Cookies

Use same recipe as Old-Fashioned Oatmeal Cookies, except omit the cinnamon and add one tablespoon grated orange rind instead and use ½ cup orange juice instead of milk. Drop from a teaspoon onto greased baking sheet. Bake at 375 degrees F for 12 to 15 minutes.

Hints: Dry orange and lemon peels and grind them to a course powder to use as flavoring for cookies, cakes, puddings, and sauces. Drop cookies can be turned into rolled cookies by kneading dough into a smooth ball on a lightly floured board. Then roll out until approximately ¼-inch thick, and cut into desired shape. For rolled cookies made from drop cookie recipes, chill dough before rolling, and roll in small portions. Save trimmings from cutting, pat together and roll again. Drop cookie dough can also be baked as bar cookies by spreading dough in pan and cutting into bars after baked. Refrigerator cookies are made from stiff dough shaped into rolls and chilled.

Cathedral Cookies

2 eggs, slightly beaten
½ cup butter
1 large package of chocolate chips
2 cups nuts, chopped
1 large package miniature marshmallows (colored)
1 teaspoon vanilla
¼ cup powdered sugar

In double boiler, cook the eggs, butter, and chocolate chips, stirring constantly until eggs appear done (doesn't take long). Add vanilla. Take off heat and cool thoroughly. Add chopped nuts and miniature marshmallows. Mix well. Then form into rolls and coat in powdered sugar. Place rolls in refrigerator until thoroughly cold (at least one hour). Slice into cookies and apply powdered sugar. Serve at room temperature. Makes about 4 twelve-inch rolls which will slice into several dozen cookies.

Christmas Cookies

2½ cups flour
1 teaspoon nutmeg
1 teaspoon cinnamon
1 teaspoon all spice
1 cup brown sugar
½ cup granulated sugar
½ cup butter
4 eggs, beaten
¼ cup milk
2 teaspoon baking soda
½ cup fruit juice (or whiskey)
1½ cups pecans, chopped
½ pound candied cherries, chopped
½ pound candied pineapple, chopped

Preheat oven to 350 degrees F. Sift together flour, nutmeg, cinnamon, and all spice. Cream brown and white sugar into butter then add eggs and beat until mixture is smooth. Add baking soda to milk and blend into sugar/egg mixture. Add pecans, cherries, and pineapple to mixture and blend in. Add fruit juice or whiskey (if desired) and mix in. Drop from teaspoon on greased cookie sheet. Bake 20 minutes in a 350 degree oven. Makes 20 dozen (240) small cookies. Enough for everyone on your Christmas list!

Orange No-Bake Cookies

¾ box powdered sugar
1 (1-pound) box vanilla wafers, crumbled
1 stick butter, melted
1 cup chopped nuts
1 6-ounce can frozen orange juice
1 (small) can/package shredded coconut

Mix all ingredients except coconut in large bowl. Shape into cookies and coat cookies in coconut. Makes 3 dozen cookies.

Other Desserts
Pineapple Sherbet
1 cup crushed pineapple
1 quart water
2 cups sugar
juice of 2 lemons
1 teaspoon of grated lemon rind

Boil sugar, water, and lemon rind together to make a syrup. Blend the syrup with the lemon juice and pineapple. Freeze.

Fruit-Gelatin Salad
1 envelop gelatin, unflavored
½ cup cold fruit juice
1 cup hot fruit juice
¼ cup sugar
¼ teaspoon salt
¼ cup lemon juice
1½ cup well drained, diced fruit

Soften gelatin in cold fruit juice. Add hot fruit juice, salt, and sugar. Sir until dissolved. Add lemon juice. Chill until mixture is semisolid. Stir in diced fruit. Pour into large or individual molds. Chill until firm. Remove from mold onto salad greens. Serves six.

Hint: Unflavored or plain gelatin comes in 1 tablespoon (1 ounce) packets. It should be softened in cold water or other liquid, then dissolved completely in hot liquid. Flavored gelatins are dissolved by adding boiling water, then any other liquid to cool.

Pink Arctic Mold

2 small packages cream cheese
2 tablespoons mayonnaise
2 tablespoons sugar
1 can whole cranberry sauce
1 9-ounce can crushed pineapple
1 cup nuts
1 cup whipping cream, whipped

Mix cream cheese, mayonnaise, and sugar well. Fold into whipped cream. Fold other ingredients into mix. Freeze.

Baked Custard

2 cups milk
2 eggs
½ cup sugar
¼ teaspoon salt
1 teaspoon vanilla extract

Heat milk to scalding in a double boiler. Beat eggs, adding sugar, salt, and vanilla until creamy. Beat in hot milk. Pour into custard cups and set cups in a pan of hot water. Bake at 325 degrees F. until firm (a toothpick inserted in center will come out clean) about 30 minutes. Cool before serving.

Banana Pudding

4 to 6 bananas, sliced thinly
1 box vanilla wafers
ingredients for Baked Custard

Preheat oven to 450 degrees F. In large baking dish or ovenproof bowl, layer vanilla wafers and banana slices until dish is full. Mix ingredients for the Baked Custard and pour custard mixture over layered wafers and bananas. Bake at 450 degrees for 10 minutes. Reduce temperature to 350 degrees and bake 30 minutes or until custard is firm. Top with meringue.

Easy Fudge

1 (8-ounce) package cream cheese
6 cups confectioners' sugar
¼ teaspoon salt
½ cup cocoa
1 teaspoon vanilla
¾ cup chopped nuts

Butter or oil a 9-inch square pan lightly. Place cream cheese in large bowl and bring to room temperature, then work with spoon until soft and smooth. Sift confectioners' sugar, salt, and coca together and blend into cream cheese until mixture is smooth and creamy. Add vanilla and nuts and blend well. Press mixture into pan and chill until firm. Cut into squares. Makes up to 24 servings.

Buttermilk Fudge

2 cups sugar
½ cup butter
1 cup buttermilk
2 tablespoons corn syrup
1 teaspoon baking soda
1 tablespoon vanilla
nutmeats, chopped (pecans, walnut, your choice)

Blend sugar into butter, then blend in buttermilk, syrup, and baking soda. Place in a pan on low heat and stir until mix dissolves. Cook, stirring, until candy mixture makes a soft ball when dropped into cold water. Cool until lukewarm, beating, then add vanilla and chopped nutmeats. Pour into a butter dish and cool. Cut into small squares.

Hints for working with chocolate: Working with chocolate is tricky since chocolate burns easily and must be watched carefully. The safest way to melt chocolate is to cut squares into small pieces, place in a small, covered bowl, and set over steaming, not boiling, water with heat turned off. Chocolate will melt as water cools.

Hints for cooked candies: Sugar changes consistency with heat. It becomes smooth at 216 degrees and thready at 220 degrees. It will form a soft ball at 240 degrees, and a hard ball at 250 degrees. Recipes generally specify "thread," "soft ball," or "hard ball." You "test" candy by dropping into a glass of cold water from the tip of a spoon.

Pecan Pralines

1½ cup pecans, halves
2½ cups brown sugar
1 cup sugar
¼ cup corn syrup
1 teaspoon vanilla
¼ teaspoon salt
1½ cups milk

Combine all ingredients except vanilla and pecans in a sauce pan, mix well, then cook, stirring constantly until it makes a soft ball when dropped into cold water. Let cool until lukewarm then add vanilla and pecan halves. Drop each pecan half coated with candy on wax paper and let cool.

Quick Spiced Peaches

1 large can cling peach halves
½ cup sugar
½ cup cider vinegar
1 tablespoon mixed pickling spices.

Drain peaches, pouring syrup from can into a large sauce pan. Add sugar, vinegar, and spices. Boil 10 minutes. Lower heat, add peach halves, and simmer for 5 minutes. Remove from heat, cover, and let fruit stand in syrup until cool. Transfer to a large jar and refrigerate until needed. Makes 2½ cups.

Quick Peach Cobbler

1 large can peaches, sliced, in syrup
½ teaspoon cinnamon
3 tablespoons cornstarch
1 cup biscuit mix (or use biscuit recipe)
3 tablespoons sugar, divided
¼ cup milk
¼ cup sour cream

Preheat oven to 400 degrees F. Drain peaches, retaining syrup. Combine syrup with cornstarch and cinnamon. Bring to a boil, reduce heat, and cook until thickened. Add peach slices and continue cooking for another two to three minutes. Pour into a baking dish. Combine biscuit mix (or biscuit recipe ingredients), 2 tablespoons of sugar, milk and sour cream to make a soft dough. Drop from a spoon into hot peach mixture. Sprinkle top with one tablespoon of sugar. Bake for 20 minutes at 400 degrees or until top is golden brown.

SOUPS

Asparagus Soup

1 pound asparagus, ends removed
1 quart water
1 teaspoon salt
¼ teaspoon pepper
1 tablespoon flour
1 tablespoon butter
2 cups milk
toasted bread, diced

Add asparagus, salt, and pepper to one quart water. Bring to boil, reduce heat, and simmer for five minutes. Remove asparagus from water, mash with a fork, then return to cooking water. Heat milk, add flour and butter, let cook for 5 minutes or until thick, then add to mashed asparagus in cooking water. Bring mixture back to a boil, reduce heat, and simmer for 10 minutes. Pour into bowls over toasted and diced bread or add croutons to top. Serves four to six.

Bean Soup

1 pound navy beans
1 ham bone
2 medium onions
4 to 6 stalks celery
2 teaspoons salt (or to taste)
1 teaspoon pepper (or to taste)
1 cup potatoes, mashed

Soak beans overnight. Drain. In enough fresh water to cover, combine beans and ham bone. Bring to boil, reduce heat, and simmer for 2 hours. Chop onions and celery into ½-inch chunks. Add to bean soup and bring back to boil. Reduce heat and simmer until beans are tender. Serves four to six.

Clam Chowder

2 cans clams (1½ cups)
2 strips bacon
4 to 6 stalks celery
2 to 3 carrots
1 onion
4 to 6 small potatoes
salt and pepper to taste
4 cups water
1 tablespoon corn starch

Drain clams, save juice, then dice clams. Fry bacon, add onion and cook until bacon is crisp and onion is tender. Dice celery, carrots, and potatoes and add with salt and pepper and clam juice to water, then stir in bacon and onion. Bring mixture to a boil, let simmer 20 minutes, then add clams. Cook another 10 minutes. For thickening, remove some of the potatoes, mash, add corn starch, then add ½ cup water to mixture. Slowly stir into chowder. Cook 3 to 5 minutes longer. Serves six.

Manhattan Clam Chowder

Add 2 cups stewed tomatoes or one can tomato soup (without additional water) to vegetable mixture.

Cream of Tomato Soup

1 can stewed tomatoes
1 cup milk
1 teaspoon butter
½ teaspoon salt
¼ teaspoon pepper

Heat tomatoes, then strain. Return to heat and add butter, salt, pepper, and thicken with flour, stirring until very thick. Heat milk separately until boiling (be careful not to scorch), then add boiling milk to tomato mixture. Serves four to six.

Corn Chowder

3 tablespoons butter
1 onion, diced
4 cups milk
salt and pepper to taste
dash cayenne
2 cups cream style corn (1 can)
3 cups potatoes, diced
4 cups water for cooking potatoes
1 tablespoon corn starch
¼ cup chopped parsley

Cook potatoes in water with salt and pepper for 20 to 30 minutes. Sauté onion in butter until brown. Add to potatoes. Drain liquid from can of corn (keeping liquid) and add kernels to mixture. Add cayenne pepper. To corn liquid, add one tablespoon corn starch, stir until smooth. Add to chowder mixture. Bring to boil, reduce heat, and simmer 5 minutes. More water can be added to achieve desired consistency. Garnish with parsley when served. Serves eight.

Cream of Onion Soup

2 medium sweet (Vidalia) onions
¼ cup butter
½ cup all-purpose flour
1 can clear chicken broth
1 cup milk
1½ cups water
½ teaspoon salt
¼ teaspoon pepper

Dice onions and sauté in butter until tender. Mix flour with chicken broth and add to onion mixture. Add milk, water, salt and pepper. Cook slowly 20 to 30 minutes. Serves six.

Chicken Soup

1 large (3 to 4 pound) chicken
2 to 3 ribs celery with leaves attached, diced
2 to 3 carrots, diced
1 onion quartered
8 whole peppercorns
1 tablespoon seasoned salt
1 (12 oz.) package wide egg noodles
4 quarts water
1 bouillon cube
1 tablespoon each parsley,
red pepper, and minced onion flakes

In a large pot, combine chicken, celery, carrot, onion, peppercorns, and seasoned salt in water. Simmer until chicken falls apart. Remove chicken from pot, cool, separate meat from skin and bone. Chop meat into small pieces. Set aside. Strain broth, pressing as much liquid from vegetables as possible through sieve, and return to pot. Bring to boil. Cook noodles in boiling broth 6 minutes. Add bouillon cube, stirring to mix well. Sir gently to dissolve lumps, yet not break noodles. Sir in chicken pieces. Add parsley flakes, red pepper flakes, minced onion flakes, pepper and additional salt if needed. Heat thoroughly. Serves six to eight.

Simple Vegetable Soup

1 each turnip, carrot, onion
3 stalks celery
2 leeks
1 teaspoon cooking oil
dash of nutmeg

Scrape vegetables and chop into ½-inch pieces, then sauté in cooking oil. Add a dash of grated nutmeg and cover with 3 pints boiling water. Simmer for one hour. Strain or blend and serve as broth. Serves four.

Hardy Vegetable Soup

Triple the quantity of vegetables for Simple Vegetable Soup and add one can of tomatoes or tomato soup, 2 small potatoes (chopped), and 2 beef bouillon cubes. Cook for 45 minutes. Don't strain vegetables from soup before serving.

Vegetable-Beef Soup

1 soup bone with meat (from roast)
4 cups water
1 medium onion, diced
3 carrots, sliced thinly
2 stalks celery, diced
1 can tomatoes
1 tablespoon salt
½ teaspoon pepper
½ pound Velveeta cheese
1 can tomato sauce

Cook soup bone in water for one to 2 hours. Add onion, carrots, and celery, and cook for 30 minutes longer. Add tomatoes, salt and pepper, and cook for 15 minutes longer. Melt cheese with tomato sauce in pan over hot water and add to soup. Heat until blended. Serves six to eight. For a more spicy blend, seed and finely chop one jalapeno pepper and add it to the Velveeta and tomato sauce blend.

Cream of Mushroom Soup

1 pound mushrooms, fresh
½ onion, sliced thinly
¼ cup butter
2 tablespoons flour
2 cups milk
2 cups water
1 teaspoon salt
½ teaspoon paprika
(directions on next page)

Clean mushrooms thoroughly. Chop or slice thinly. Slice onions. Heat butter in saucepan and sauté mushrooms and onions. Add flour and blend well. Add milk and one cup water, stirring constantly until thickened. Bring to boil and simmer for 2 minutes. Add more water as necessary to obtain desired texture. Add salt and paprika. Serve hot garnished with chopped parsley. Serves four to six.

Baked Potato Soup

4 large potatoes
½ cup butter
½ cup flour
1½ quarts milk
½ teaspoon salt
¼ teaspoon pepper
4 green onions, chopped
1 cup sour cream
2 cups crisply cooked bacon, crumbled
4 ounces cheddar cheese, grated
2 teaspoon chives, chopped

Reserve a little of the crumbled bacon, cheese, and chives for garnish. Bake potatoes until fork tender. Cut potatoes in half, scoop out meat, and set aside. Chop half of the potato peels and discard remainder. Melt butter in saucepan. Slowly blend flour in butter, then gradually add milk to the butter-flour mixture stirring constantly. Add salt and pepper and simmer over low heat, stirring. Add potatoes, green onions, and potato peels, then sour cream and crumbled bacon. Heat thoroughly. Add cheese a little at a time until all is melted in. Garnish with chives, grated cheese, and bacon crumbles. Serves eight.

Tortilla Soup

1 small green bell pepper
1 yellow onion
½ pound celery
½ pound carrots
½ cup cilantro leaves
1 tablespoon minced garlic
2 teaspoons each chili powder and cumin
1½ teaspoons cracked black peppercorns
2 sticks plus 2 tablespoons butter, divided
½ cup olive oil
10 ounces corn tortillas
3 quarts water
1 cup chicken stock
½ cup flour
1¼ pounds tomatoes, peeled and coarsely chopped
2 pounds skinless, boneless chicken breasts, cooked, diced
5 tortillas (cut into 1/8- by 1-inch strips)
Grated cheddar cheese for garnish

Clean, peel, and dice the bell pepper, onion, celery, carrots, and cilantro. Combine garlic, chili powder, cumin, and pepper, and add to vegetables. Melt one stick plus 2 tablespoons butter in a large pan over medium heat. Add olive oil and vegetables and sauté, stirring often, until vegetables are transparent and lightly browned. Chop tortillas into ½-inch pieces and add to vegetable mixture. Continue cooking over medium heat until tortillas are soft. Transfer mixture to a large pot and add water and chicken stock. In a large skillet, melt remaining one stick butter and whisk in flour. Cook 2 to 3 minutes, while whisking, to make a roux. Add roux to soup mixture, stir, and let soup simmer 20 minutes. Sir in chopped tomatoes and diced chicken. Cook five minutes more. Ladle soup into bowls and sprinkle with tortilla strips and grated cheese. Makes approximately one gallon soup.

SALADS

Bride's Fruit Salad

1 large can chunk pineapple
1 large can pears
1 large can white cherries
½ pound almonds
½ pound small marshmallows
½ cup milk
4 eggs, yolks only
juice of 1 lemon
¼ teaspoon prepared mustard
2 cups whipped cream

Drain and combine the fruit. Chop nuts. Combine nuts and marshmallows with fruit. Combine milk, egg yolks, lemon juice, and mustard in a double boiler and cook over hot water until mixture thickens. Cool. Fold 2 cups whipped cream into mixture. Blend in fruit, nuts, and marshmallow mixture. Refrigerator at least 2 hours before serving. Serve on salad greens. Serves six.

Sauerkraut Slaw

1 large can shredded sauerkraut
1 medium onion
1 medium bell pepper, seeded
1 cup sugar

Dice onions and bell pepper. Drain sauerkraut. Combine onions, bell peppers, sauerkraut, and sugar. Mix well and turned into a covered dish. Cover and refrigerate at least 12 hour before serving. Serve as a relish or a salad with a meat dishes. Serves four to six.

Chicken Salad

2 cups cooked chicken
1½ cups celery
5 egg yolks, beaten
½ cup butter
1 teaspoon salt
1 teaspoon mustard
black or red pepper to taste
1 cup whipped cream
1 tablespoon lemon juice
7 tablespoons vinegar
2 teaspoons vinegar
nuts, chopped (if desired)

Dressing: Boil 7 tablespoons vinegar in double boiler, whisk in egg yolks and heat until smooth. Slowly mix in butter, salt, pepper, and mustard. Remove from heat and cool. Add 2 teaspoons cold vinegar, lemon juice, and whipped cream. Mix well. Let set for 10 minutes while you chop chicken and celery into small (¼-inch) pieces. Add to dressing mixture. Add nuts (optional). Serve over bed of greens. **Variation:** add chopped salad greens to mixture and serve in a scooped out tomato. Serves six.

Pea-Cheese Salad

2 cups small peas (drain if canned peas are used)
1 cup celery
1 onion
½ cup sweet pickles
1 cup cheese (your choice), grated
2 tablespoons mayonnaise
salt and pepper to taste

Dice celery, onion, and pickles. Blend all ingredients. Additional mayonnaise can be added to moisten. Chill, then serve. Serves six to eight.

Caesar Salad

½ to 1 head lettuce
1 bunch curly endive
2 tomatoes, diced
1 tomato, sliced thinly
1 cup croutons
1 clove garlic, mashed
½ cup olive oil
¼ cup lemon juice
1 egg, beaten
½ cup Parmesan cheese, grated
¼ cup bleu cheese, finely crumbled
1 teaspoon Worcestershire sauce
¼ teaspoon pepper
½ teaspoon salt

Combine garlic and olive oil; let stand. Combine lettuce, endive, tomatoes, and half the croutons. Combine remaining ingredients with garlic and olive oil, mix well, and pour over salad. Toss lightly. Garnish with sliced tomatoes and remaining croutons. Serves six. **Variation:** Add ½ cup diced ham or add ¼ cup crumbled anchovies to the mixture.

Tossed Vegetable-Cheese Salad

1 head lettuce
1 green pepper
4 to 5 stalks celery
1 onion (red, if available)
1 package frozen green peas, thawed
1 cup cheddar cheese, shredded
1 cup salad dressing

Tear lettuce into small pieces. Dice green pepper and celery. Slice onion thinly. Toss vegetables and cheese, add salad dressing (or mayonnaise) to moisten. Serves six to eight.

Pineapple-Cheese Salad

½ pound grated cheese (your choice)
1 large can crushed pineapple
1 cup pineapple juice (use can juice)
1½ tablespoons vinegar
2 tablespoons flour
1 egg, beaten
½ cup sugar

Drain pineapple, reserve juice. Combine pineapple with grated cheese and set aside. Combine juice, vinegar, flour, egg, sugar, and pineapple juice in sauce pan and cook over slow heat until thick. Pour over cheese/pineapple mix while hot. Stir lightly to combine. Serves four to six as side dish.

24-Hour Slaw

1 head cabbage
1 onion
2 sweet green peppers, seeded
½ cup olives
1 cup sugar
½ cup vinegar
½ cup vegetable oil
1 teaspoon mustard
1 teaspoon celery seed
salt and pepper to taste

Chop cabbage into ½-inch pieces. Dice onion, green peppers. Slice olives. Combine cabbage, onion, green peppers, and olives in large bowl with ½ cup sugar. Combine in a saucepan: ½ cup sugar, vinegar, vegetable oil, mustard, celery seed, and salt. Bring to a boil and simmer for 8 to 10 minutes. Pour over cabbage mixture while hot. Chill for 24 hours before serving. Serves six to eight as side dish.

Southwestern Tossed Salad
Salad greens and vegetables of your choice
2 avocados

To salad greens and other fresh vegetables of your choice, add peeled and sliced avocados. Top with cilantro dressing.

Potato Salad
2 cups cooked potatoes
1 cup celery
1 onion
½ cup mayonnaise or salad dressing
1 tablespoon vinegar
2 teaspoon salt
½ teaspoon pepper
2 hardboiled eggs, sliced

Dice cooked potatoes, celery, and onion. Toss together with half of the hardboiled eggs. Stir in mayonnaise or salad dressing plus 1 tablespoon vinegar. Use the remaining hardboiled eggs as garnish. Serves six.

Three-Bean Salad
2 cups (or cans) wax beans
2 cups (or cans) red kidney beans
2 cups (or cans) green beans, chopped short
1 onion, chopped fine
½ cup vinegar
½ cup salad oil
½ cup sugar
½ teaspoon salt
¼ teaspoon pepper

Drain and mix all beans. Combine all other ingredients, mixing well, then add to beans and blend together. Refrigerate overnight before serving. Serves eight as side dish.

DRESSINGS & SAUCES

Mayonnaise

2 egg yolks
1 teaspoon salt
1 teaspoon sugar
1 teaspoon dry mustard
¼ teaspoon paprika
dash of cayenne pepper
1 tablespoon vinegar and 3 tablespoons lemon juice
(or 5 tablespoons lemon juice)
2 cups olive oil
1 tablespoon hot water

Beat egg yolks until thick. Add salt, sugar, dry mustard, paprika, cayenne and continue beating. Add oil and vinegar or lemon juice a few drops at a time until mixture begins to thicken, then add oil more rapidly. Beat in 1 tablespoon hot water. Store in covered container in refrigerator. Makes about two cups mayonnaise.

Horseradish Sauce

8-ounce package cream cheese
1 tablespoon sugar
2 to 3 tablespoons prepared horseradish
1 teaspoon lemon juice
1 teaspoon Worcestershire sauce
¼ cup whipping cream, whipped

Soften cream cheese by letting it come to room temperature. Fold in other ingredients. Blend until smooth. Makes 2 cups.

Cilantro Dressing

1 bunch cilantro
2 tablespoons garlic
2 tablespoons jalapeno peppers, seeded
¼ cup white wine vinegar
¼ cup water
2 cups mayonnaise
½ teaspoon salt

Blend/purée cilantro, garlic, jalapenos, vinegar, water, and salt together. Fold into mayonnaise. Chill. Makes two cups. Decrease amount of water and vinegar for a dip.

Cooked Salad Dressing

1 tablespoon butter
2 tablespoons flour
½ teaspoon salt
½ teaspoon dry mustard
1 tablespoon sugar
½ cup water
1 egg yolk
¼ teaspoon paprika
½ cup olive oil
2 tablespoons lemon juice

Melt butter in top of double boiler. Blend in flour, salt, dry mustard, and sugar. Gradually add water. Cook, stirring until thickened. Add egg yolk and paprika to olive oil and beat until smooth. Add lemon juice and continue beating until smooth and creamy. Makes about 1½ cups salad dressing.

Blue Cheese Dressing

2 ounces crumbled bleu cheese
1 cup mayonnaise
Combine blue cheese and mayonnaise and mix well.

Tangy French Dressing

½ cup vinegar
2 tablespoons onion juice or minced onion
2 tablespoons garlic, minced
1 teaspoon salt
¼ teaspoon pepper
1 tablespoon Worcestershire sauce
½ cup catsup
3 cups olive or vegetable oil

Add vinegar, onion, garlic, salt and pepper, Worcestershire sauce, catsup, and any other spices or seasoning desired. Pour into bottle and add oil. Shake until well blended.

Western Dressing

1 cup mayonnaise
½ cup dairy sour cream
½ cup snipped fresh parsley
3 tablespoons snipped fresh chives
3 tablespoons tarragon vinegar
1 tablespoon lemon juice
dash of pepper.

Combine all ingredients. Blend until smooth. Chill.

Whipped Onion-Garlic Butter

¼ cup butter or margarine
1 teaspoon Worcestershire sauce
¼ teaspoon dry mustard
¼ teaspoon cracked pepper
2 tablespoons each minced onion, garlic, and parsley

Cream butter or margarine, Worcestershire sauce, and dry mustard together until fluffy. Sir in pepper, onions, garlic and parsley. Serve on bread, potatoes, or roast beef.

Western Vegetable Dip

1 cup mayonnaise
1 cup catsup
½ cup lemon juice
1 tablespoon dry mustard
2 tablespoons horseradish sauce
1 tablespoon sugar
1 teaspoon Worcestershire sauce
¼ teaspoon pepper
½ teaspoon salt
1 jalapeno pepper (optional), seeded and diced

Combine all ingredients and blend well. Chill until thickened. Keep in tightly closed container in refrigerator.

Cheese Dip

1 cup cream cheese
1 cup bleu cheese
1 green pepper, diced
¼ teaspoon garlic salt
1 teaspoon celery seed
½ cup evaporated milk

Combine all ingredients, blend well, then beat until fluffy. Chill before serving.

Crab Dip

1 pounds crab meat
1 cups mayonnaise
1 onion, diced
1 cup cheese, grated
1 dash Worcestershire sauce
½ cup sherry wine

Mix all ingredients except cheese. Place in a baking dish, sprinkle cheese on top, and bake at 350 degrees F for 15 minutes.

Simple Mustard Dip

½ cup mayonnaise
2 tablespoons prepared mustard
(or 2 teaspoons dry mustard)
3 tablespoons cream
2 teaspoons lemon juice
1 teaspoon Worcestershire sauce
dash hot sauce

Combine all ingredients, blend well. Chill before using.

Cranberry Sauce

2 cups cranberries, cleaned
1½ cups sugar
1½ cups boiling water

Combine cranberries, sugar, and boiling water in saucepan over medium heat, stirring mixture until it comes to a boil. Reduce heat and cook slowly one hour. Pour into a mold or serving bowl and chill until firm (best to refrigerate over night). Serve with roast poultry and dressing.

Cranberry Frappé

2 cups cranberries
1½ cups sugar
1½ cups boiling water
½ cup cold water
2 tablespoons lemon juice
½ tablespoon gelatin

Combine cranberries, sugar, and 1½ cup boiling water in sauce pan, stirring mixture until it comes to a boil. Cook cranberries until soft, approximately one hour. Remove from heat and add lemon juice. Soak gelatin in cold water. Blend into cooked cranberries. Turn into a shallow dish and freeze. Scoop out into serving dish and serve with roast turkey.

VEGETABLE SIDE DISHES

Asparagus Loaf

1 pound cooked fresh asparagus (or 2 cups canned)
1 egg
1 cup milk, heated
1 cup whole wheat cracker or bread crumbs
1 tablespoon melted butter
1 teaspoon minced onion
½ teaspoon salt
¼ teaspoon pepper
¼ to ½ pound bacon, fried

Preheat oven to 350 degrees F. Cook fresh asparagus in 1 cup water for no more than 10 minutes and cut into 1-inch pieces. Beat egg slightly, add heated milk gradually. Add cracker or bread crumbs, butter, onion, and salt and pepper. Let stand a few minutes until the crumbs absorb the liquid. If additional liquid is necessary, use asparagus juice from cooking or can. Fold the asparagus into the mixture carefully. Bake in a 350 degree oven for 30 minutes. Serve with a cream sauce and garnish with crisp strips of bacon.

Carrot Fritters

2 cups carrots
2 eggs, beaten
2 tablespoons flour
1 tablespoon sugar
butter or olive oil to cover bottom of pan

Cook carrots until tender in 2 cups water, drain, then mash. Add eggs, flour, and sugar. Mix thoroughly and drop from spoon into hot butter or oil. Fry until brown.

Baked Beans

1 pound dried beans (navy or kidney)
1 medium onion, sliced
½ cup catsup
¼ cup mustard
½ pound salt pork (can substitute bacon)
2 tablespoons dark brown sugar
salt and pepper to taste

Wash beans thoroughly and soak overnight. Use same water to cook beans until tender. Pour liquid from beans. (Use some beans and liquid to make a bean soup for another meal.) Mix remaining beans with catsup, mustard, pork or bacon, brown sugar, salt and pepper. Place in casserole dish and fold in most of sliced onions, leaving some to sprinkle over top. Bake beans for two hours at 300 degrees F. Liquid from drained beans can be added during baking if too dry.

Creamed Carrots

1 pound package of carrots
1 cup water
½ teaspoon salt
2 tablespoons butter
2 tablespoons flour
1 cup milk
½ cup parsley, chopped

Peel and slice carrots into rounds. Cook carrots in water with salt. Mix butter, flour, and milk in bowl. Stir into carrots and bring to boil. Sprinkle with chopped parsley just before serving. Serves six to eight as a side dish.

Sweet Creamed Carrots

Add 2 tablespoons of sugar to butter/flour/milk mixture in creamed carrots recipe above. Serves six to eight as side dish.

Quick Potato Casserole

One two-pound bag frozen hash brown potatoes
¼ teaspoon salt
1 cup cream of chicken soup
1 pint sour cream
1 small onion chopped
10 ounces cheddar cheese, grated
½ cup bread crumbs
(or crumbled cereal such as Rice Chex)
¼ cup butter, melted

Thaw frozen hash brown potatoes. Mix all ingredients except crumbs and butter together. Pour into 3-quart baking dish. Bake 1 to 1½ hours at 350 degrees F. Sprinkle on topping of crumbs or Rice Chex in melted butter. Serves eight.

Eggplant au Gratin

1 eggplant
4 tablespoons butter
½ cup cheddar cheese
1 cup milk
½ teaspoon paprika
salt and pepper to taste

Peel and slice eggplant. Salt and pepper eggplant lightly, then fry in butter until tender. Place in shallow baking dish. Combine cheese, milk, paprika in the top of a double boiler and stir until perfectly smooth. Cover eggplant with cheese sauce. Brown under broiler or in oven. Serves four to six.

Asparagus with Sour Cream Sauce
1 to 1½ pounds fresh asparagus
1 cup sour cream
1 yolk from boiled egg, crumbled

Cook asparagus in small amount of salted water until just tender. Drain. Garnished with sour cream and egg yolks.

Baked Cabbage
1 medium firm white cabbage
2 eggs, well beaten
1 tablespoon butter
salt and pepper to taste
3 tablespoons cream

Clean and boil cabbage for fifteen minutes, then change water and bring to boil again. Cook 10 minutes, drain water, and set cabbage aside to cool. When cold, dice cabbage and add two eggs, butter, salt and pepper, and cream. Pour into a well-buttered casserole dish and bake until top is brown. Serves six.

Creamed String Beans
1 cup cooked or canned string beans
1 egg yolk
½ cup milk
½ teaspoon lemon juice
¼ teaspoon salt

Heat beans with a little hot water or can juice if not freshly cooked. Drain off excess liquid. Beat the egg yolk, add milk, and cook in double boiler until mixture begins to thicken. Add juice of lemon slowly, stirring constantly. Then add salt and string beans and mix well. Serve hot. Serves six.

French Style Green Peas

2 cups fresh or frozen peas
1 onion, diced
1 head lettuce, cut into thin strips
1 sprig of mint, diced
1 sprig of parsley, diced
1 teaspoon sugar
2 tablespoon milk
½ teaspoon salt

Combine peas, onions, lettuce, mint, parsley, and sugar in saucepan. Add enough water to cover and cook peas until tender. Add milk and salt. Stir, cook 2 minutes, and serve.

Corn Fritters

1 can whole kernel corn, drained
1 teaspoon salt
1 tablespoon sugar
2 eggs, beaten
½ cup flour
2 tablespoons baking powder

Mix all ingredients together and drop by spoonfuls into deep hot fat and fry. Serves six to eight.

Fried Cucumbers

2 large cucumbers, peeled and sliced
salt and pepper to taste
1 egg, beaten
½ cup cracker crumbs
¼ cup olive oil

Mix salt and pepper with cracker crumbs. Dip cucumber slices into beaten egg, then into cracker crumbs. Fry in olive oil until brown on each side. Serve with chili sauce.

Fried Okra

1 pound fresh okra, sliced into ½-inch pieces
(or bag of frozen okra)
salt and pepper to taste
¼ cup flour
¼ cup cornmeal
¼ cup butter or olive oil

Mix flour, cornmeal, salt, and pepper. Coat sliced okra in flour/cornmeal mixture. Fry in butter or oil until brown. Serves six.

Fried Eggplant

1 medium size eggplant
2 teaspoons salt
1 cup water
½ cup cooking oil
1 egg, beaten
½ cup flour or ½ cup bread crumbs

Peel and slice eggplant into ¼-inch slices. Soak in water and salt mixture for one-half hour. Drain. Dry pieces on paper towel. Dip in egg then in crumbs or flour. Fry in oil until brown. Serves six.

Cheese Carrots

2 cups round-sliced cooked carrots
1 cup grated Cheddar cheese
3 tablespoons butter
1 cup fine bread crumbs

Layer carrots, cheese, dots of butter, and crumbs in a casserole dish. Bake at 350 degrees for 20 minutes. Serves six.

Fried Tomatoes with Thyme and Garlic
4 tablespoons olive oil
6 to 8 firm tomatoes
4 tablespoons fresh thyme leaves
2 garlic cloves
1 teaspoon sea salt

Heat oil in skillet. Core tomatoes and cut in half from top to bottom. Add tomatoes to oil in skillet with skin down. Cook until skin is dark brown, about 4 minutes. Turn and cook until the cut side is dark brown. Reduce heat and continue cooking, turning tomatoes, until they are dark around edges and have almost melted, about 15. When tomatoes are cooked, transfer to serving dish and sprinkle with salt. Just before serving, mince thyme and garlic together and sprinkle over tomatoes.

Golden Onion Rings
4 to 6 medium onions
2 tablespoons all-purpose flour
½ teaspoon salt
1 egg, slightly beaten
1 cup milk
2 tablespoons salad oil

Slice onions ½-inch thick and separate rings. Combine flour, salt, egg, milk, and salad oil and beat until a smooth batter. Coat onion rings with batter. Deep fry, a few at a time, in hot fat (375 degrees F), stirring as needed to separate rings. When onions are a golden brown, remove and drain on paper towels. Sprinkle with salt and serve hot.

Mashed Potatoes

2 eggs, boiled
6 to 8 medium potatoes
¼ cup butter
1 cup milk
½ teaspoon salt
¼ teaspoon pepper
¼ cup onions, diced
¼ cup parsley, diced

Boil eggs, shell, slice thinly, and set aside. Peel and dice potatoes, then cook potatoes in saucepan with sufficient water to cover, adding salt and pepper to taste, 20 to 30 minutes or until tender. Remove from heat, drain water from potatoes and set water aside. Add butter and milk to potatoes and mash until they are smooth (the set aside potato water can be used to thin if needed). Stir in onions and half of the egg slices. Heap into serving dish. Garnish with parsley and remaining egg slices.

New Potatoes

10 to 12 small new (red skin) potatoes
1 teaspoon salt
½ teaspoon pepper
¼ cup butter
2 medium cloves garlic, diced
¼ cup parsley, diced

Cook unpeeled potatoes until tender but firm (20 to 30 minutes) with salt and pepper. Remove from heat and chop. Sauté garlic in butter. Add potatoes and toss to cover with butter/garlic. Garnish with parsley. Serves six to eight.

Stuffed Eggplant

2 small eggplants
1 cup ham, minced
1 to 2 small onions, finely chopped
3 tablespoons grated bread crumbs
2 tablespoons butter
1 teaspoon salt
¼ teaspoon pepper

Cut eggplants into halves. Scrape out insides and put into saucepan with minced ham. Cover with water and boil until tender. Drain water from pan. Add bread crumbs, one tablespoon butter, and salt and pepper to taste to eggplant and mix well. Stuff hull halves with mixture. Add a small lump of butter to each and bake fifteen minutes.

Stuffed Mushrooms

1 pound large mushrooms
3 tablespoons butter
1 tablespoon grated onion
½ cup fine, soft bread crumbs
1 tablespoon parsley, diced
¼ teaspoon salt
2 tablespoons catsup

Wash mushrooms, remove stems and dice stems. Melt butter in skillet, add mushroom stems and onion, and sauté. Add crumbs, parsley, salt, and catsup and mix well. Stuff mushroom caps with mixture, place in baking pan, add ¼ cup water, and bake at 350 degrees F for 15 minutes.

Cheese Noodle Ring

1 pound package of noodles
3 tablespoons butter
1 teaspoon salt
2 cups Cheddar cheese, shredded
2 teaspoons Worchestershire sauce

Cook noodles in boiling salted water until tender. Drain. Add butter to noodles. Toss until butter has melted then pour into a ring mold. Place mold in a pan of hot water and bake at 350 degrees F for 25 minutes. Melt cheddar cheese, stirring in Worchestershire sauce. Unmold noodles onto plate and pour cheese sauce over noodle ring.

Spanish Rice

1½ cups rice
1 pound ground beef
½ cup onion, diced
½ cup green pepper, diced
1 can tomatoes
½ cup tomato catsup
2 teaspoons salt
½ teaspoon pepper
¼ to ½ teaspoon chilli powder
1 beef bouillon cube
2 cups hot water

Prepare rice according to package direction, adding one beef bouillon cube. Brown ground beef in a skillet and drain grease from pan. Add green pepper and onion to pan and sauté with ground beef. Combine rice, tomatoes, tomato catsup, hot water, and salt, pepper, chilli powder and add to ingredients in skillet. Stir until all moisture is absorbed. Mix skillet ingredients with rice and place in baking dish. Baked at 350 degrees F for 30 minutes, stirring occasionally, adding water as needed. Serves eight.

Sweet Potatoes with Pineapple

3 medium sized sweet potatoes, baked
1 can crushed pineapple
2 tablespoons butter
2 tablespoons sugar
pinch of salt

Bake sweet potatoes until soft (about 30 minutes), cool, slice lengthwise, scoop out center, and cream with butter, sugar, salt. Drain juice from can of pineapple and mix fruit with creamed potatoes. Fill shells with mixture and sprinkle a little crushed pineapple over top. Brown lightly and serve.

Stuffed Onions

6 large onions
½ cup green pepper
2 stalks celery
2 to 4 sprigs fresh parsley
1 teaspoon salt
¼ teaspoon pepper
12 butter crackers, finely crumbled

Remove onion skins. Boil onions in salted water for 5 minutes. Drain and place in cold water. Cut in half crosswise, place back into pan and simmer in more salted water until almost tender. Drain again. Remove centers of onions and chop finely with green peppers, celery, and parsley, then stuff onions. Bake covered at 425 degrees F for 45 minutes.

Turnip Greens with Hog Jowl

1½ pounds turnip greens (1 to 2 large bunches)
1 tablespoon salt
1 pound hog jowl or ham hock
2 to 3 cups water
(directions on next page)

Place meat in soup pot, add salt and enough water to cover. Simmer until meat is tender (about 1 hour). Add greens and simmer about 15 minutes. Drain. Serves six to eight.

Baked Corn

1 can cream style corn
½ cup milk
1 egg, beaten
¼ cup sugar
2 tablespoons flour
salt and pepper to taste

Combine all ingredients, blend well. Pour into baking dish and bake at 350 degrees F for 45 to 60 minutes.

Scalloped Tomatoes

4 to 6 medium tomatoes, sliced
½ teaspoon salt
¼ teaspoon pepper
2 tablespoons butter
¼ cup sugar
½ cup bread crumbs

Preheat oven to 350 degrees F. Grease a small baking dish, layer bottom with bread crumbs, then add a layer of sliced tomatoes, sprinkled with salt and pepper, bits of butter, and sugar. Repeat layering with crumbs and tomatoes, butter, and sugar until pan is full, with a top layer of tomatoes. Sprinkled top with crumbs. Place a bit of butter on each top slice. Bake covered for 20 to 25 minutes in a 350 degree oven. Serves four to six as side dish.

PICKLES & RELISHES

Curtido/Carrot Relish
1 pound carrots
¼ to ½ cup sliced onion
3 ounces canned jalapenos, whole or sliced
¼ cup each: water and vegetable oil
2 cups white vinegar
2 ounces arbol chilies, cleaned
1 teaspoon oregano
1 teaspoon cumin (cominos)
1 teaspoon basil
1 teaspoon black pepper
1 teaspoon salt
2 tablespoons sugar

Thinly slice onions and carrots. Bring water, oil, and vinegar to a boil in large saucepan. Reduce heat, add chilies and simmer 5 minutes. Add oregano, cominos, basil, pepper, salt, and sugar and cook an additional 5 minutes. Add carrots and onion and cook 10 minutes or to desired texture. Add jalapenos and simmer 5 minutes. Cool, then refrigerate.

Dilly Cucumbers
1 large cucumber
½ cup salad oil
3 tablespoons vinegar
1½ teaspoon snipped dill or ½ teaspoon dried dill weed
¼ teaspoon each sugar, salt, and teaspoon pepper

Peel and slice cucumber thinly. Beat oil and vinegar together and add other ingredients. Pour mixture over cucumber. Refrigerate for several hours.

Marinated Artichoke Hearts

1 (large) can artichoke hearts
2 cups white wine vinegar
2 cups water
4 dried bay leaves
10 peppercorns
2 allspice berries
1 garlic clove
2 cups olive oil
2 branches fresh rosemary
(or 1 teaspoon dried leaves)
2 dried bay leaves

Place vinegar and water in a saucepan and add artichoke hearts, bay leaves, peppercorns, and allspice. Bring to boil, reduce heat, and cook about 3 minutes. Transfer the hearts to a tea towel and pat dry. Thinly slice the garlic clove lengthwise. Break the rosemary stems to fit jar. Cut the hearts in quarters and place in 3 to 4 pint glass jars, alternating artichokes and garlic. Completely cover with olive oil. Add rosemary stems and bay leaves and close the jars. Place jars in a dark place for at least 3 days before serving—the artichokes improve with age and will keep for several months. Makes about 2 cups. Reuse leftover oil for salads.

Tomato Preserves

8 cups tomatoes
4 cups sugar
½ lemon, sliced thin
1 teaspoon cinnamon
1 quart water

Scald tomatoes and peel. Cut into chunks and boil with sugar and cinnamon for about one hour or until thick. Put in scalded clean, hot jar. Makes about 4 pints.

Bread and Butter Pickles
12 large cucumbers
6 to 8 onions
1 quart vinegar
4 cups sugar
2 tablespoons prepared mustard
¼ teaspoon cinnamon
1 teaspoon tumeric powder
½ teaspoon nutmeg
½ teaspoon red pepper
6 sprigs of dill

Slice cucumbers into ¼-inch rounds or lengthwise into eights and soak them in salt water one hour. Drain, then add vinegar, sugar, cinnamon, mustard, tumeric, nutmeg, and red pepper mixture. Bring to boil and simmer 30 minutes. Pour into sterilized pint jars, add a sprig of dill, and seal while hot. Makes 8 pints. Refrigerate after opening.

Easy Corn Relish
1 tablespoon cornstarch
¼ cup water
1½ cups (1 can) whole kernel corn, undrained
½ cup sugar
½ cup vinegar
1 teaspoon tumeric
1 onion, finely chopped
½ teaspoon celery seed
¼ teaspoon red pepper

In saucepan, blend cornstarch and water. Add remaining ingredients. Cook and stir over medium heat until mixture thickens. Makes 2 cups (1 pint). Refrigerate to store.

Hot Chow-Chow

2 dozen cucumbers
1½ dozen bell peppers
1 bunch carrots
3 to 4 heads cabbage
1 dozen onions
3 dozen green tomatoes
1 pound green beans (parboil 10 minutes)
6 hot green jalapeno peppers
3 cups salt
water to cover

Clean vegetables, chop into ½-inch or smaller pieces, and soak overnight in salted water. Next morning, combine the following and bring to a boil:

½ gallon vinegar
3 tablespoons dry mustard
3 tablespoons mustard seed
1 quart (4 cups) water
1 tablespoon celery seed
1 tablespoon tumeric powder

Drain salted water from vegetables and add vegetables to the boiling liquid. (If not enough liquid, make more in same proportions.) Boil 15 minutes. Spoon into sterile pint jars and seal. Makes about 12 to 16 pints (24 to 32 cups, 6 to 8 quarts, 1½ to 2 gallons). Refrigerate after opening.

Hint: If you can't use this much chow-chow, reduce recipe proportions to something more manageable (I'd do the math, but it's just too overwhelming) or give jars as gifts.

Watermelon Rind Preserves

2 to 4 pounds of rind from a ripe watermelon
1 pound sugar
1 cup vinegar
1 lemon, sliced and seeded
1 teaspoon grated lemon rind
2 quarts water (approximate)
1 teaspoon ground cinnamon
1 stick cinnamon per jar

Cut the watermelon rind into 1-inch strips, remove green outer rind and any red melon remaining, then chop into 1-inch pieces. Place rind pieces in soup kettle and cover with water. Boil until rind is tender and transparent (about one hour). Drain and rinse in clear water, then return to kettle. In another pan, boil one quart water, sugar, lemon slices, lemon rind, and ground cinnamon together for 15 to 20 minutes to make a light syrup. Remove from heat, pour over rinds, and refrigerate overnight. Pour off syrup and boil it until it is very thick. Pack rinds in sterile jars. Add one stick cinnamon per jar and pour in boiling syrup to cover. Seal jars. Refrigerate after opening.

Dill Pickles

12 to 16 cucumbers
4 cups water
1 cup vinegar
½ cup salt
4 to 6 sprigs dill

Slice cucumbers lengthwise, place in sterile canning jars, and add a sprig of dill. Bring water, vinegar, salt, and one dill sprig to boil. Pour boiling mixture over cucumbers. Seal jars. Wait one week to use. Refrigerate after opening.

JAMS & JELLIES

Orange Marmalade
4 oranges
2 lemons
1 quarts water
2 pounds sugar

Slice oranges and lemons thinly. Remove seeds. Place oranges and lemon slices in kettle with water. Refrigerate for 48 hours then boil for 2 hours. Add sugar and let boil an additional two hours. Pour into jelly glasses and seal.

Jelly-making Hint: To test jelly, cool a spoonful of mixture slightly then drip from edged of spoon. If it runs like syrup, jelly is not cooked enough. If it breaks off in flakes or sheets, the jelly stage has been reached. To prevent mold, always pour boiling hot jelly or jam into sterilized jars and seal with sterilized lids. Refrigerate after opening. Discard any jellies or jams which grow a mold on surface since they may contain mycotoxins harmful to humans and animals.

Jalapeno Pepper Jelly
1 cup green sweet peppers, ground
¼ cup jalapeno peppers, ground
6 cups sugar
1½ cups apple cider vinegar
1 bottle liquid fruit pectin

Mix all. Bring to a full rolling boil. Boil one minute. Remove from heat. Add bottle of liquid pectin. Stir well. Add a few drops of green food coloring. Pour into clean jelly glasses and seal with sterile lid. Refrigerate after opening.

Grape Jelly
2 pounds white or Concord grapes
1 pound sugar
1 quart water
1 package powdered fruit pectin

Pick over grapes carefully to remove "overripe" fruit. Mash and pour all into a large kettle containing one quart water. Cook slowly for ten minutes. Strain through a colander and return juice to kettle. Add one package pectin. Boil rapidly for 25 minutes, remove from heat and pour into sterile jelly glasses. Seal with sterile jar lids. Refrigerate after opening.

Pineapple-Cherry Jam
1 large can crushed pineapple
9-ounce jar Marichino cherries
juice of ½ lemon
1 package of powdered fruit pectin
6 cups sugar
4 cups water

Measure and set aside sugar. Chop cherries and add to crushed pineapple and lemon juice. Add water and package of pectin to mixture and bring to full rolling boil, stirring constantly. While boiling, add sugar all at once. Bring back to boil and boil 10 minutes, stirring constantly. Let set for one minute. Skim. Add a few drops of red food coloring and stir. Pour into scalded clean jelly jars. Stir a few times to prevent fruit from settling as jam cools. Seal with sterile jar lids. Refrigerate after opening.

Strawberry Jam
4 cups Sugar
6 cups Stawberries
½ teaspoon butter
3 ounces liquid pectin

Wash and hull strawberries, then measure. Place berries and sugar into a stainless kettle, mix well, and refrigerate overnight. Place on medium high heat, add butter and pectin, and cook about ten minutes. Pour into sterilized jelly glasses and seal.

Blackberry Jam

3 cups blackberries (fresh, cleaned)
6 cups sugar
4 cups water
1 package powdered fruit pectin

Combine berries, sugar, water, and package of pectin. Bring to boil and boil 15 minutes, stirring constantly. Pour into sterile jars, stir a few times to prevent fruit from settling as it cools, and seal with sterile lids. Refrigerate after opening.

Plum Jelly

4 cups (1 quart) plums
4 cups water
4 cups sugar
1 package powdered fruit pectin

Add plums to water in large sauce pan. Boil until plums are soft. Pour through strainer, sieving out pulp, peels and pit. Return juice to sauce pan. Add sugar and package of pectin and boil 20 minutes. Pour into sterile jars and seal with sterile lids. Refrigerate after opening.

Plum Marmalade

pulp and peels from previous recipe
equal amount of sugar
1 package powdered fruit pectin

Press pulp and peels through a colander. Add an equal amount of sugar as pulp and peels and package of pectin. Boil 20 minutes. Pour into sterile jars and seal. Refrigerate.

Beverages
Syrup
3 cups sugar
1½ cups water

Combine sugar and water and bring to boil. Boil 10 minutes. Cool. Pour into clean jar and cover. Refrigerate. Use to sweeten beverages or on pancakes.

Lemonade
5 to 6 lemons
1 cup sugar syrup or 5 to 6 cups sugar
3½ cups water

Slice lemons into two halves, squeeze, and strain juice. Mix juice, sugar syrup or sugar, and water. Refrigerate/chill. Before serving, pour over ice cubes in glass and garnish with fresh fruit and mint. Makes about one quart. Additional water can be added for less tart taste.

Fruit Punch
4 cups grape juice
2 cups orange juice
1½ cups lemon juice
2 cups ginger ale
8 cups water

Combine chilled grape, orange, and lemon juices, ginger ale, and water. Add sugar to taste. Stir. Let stand in tightly covered container in refrigerator for one hour. Pour into punch bowl, add ice cubes. Garnish with orange slices.

Ching-a-ling Float
1 cup boiling water
1½ cup sugar
3 cups orange juice
1½ teaspoon peppermint extract
½ pint vanilla ice cream
fresh mint leaves

Pour boiling water over sugar and stir until dissolved. Chill. Combine orange juice and peppermint extract. Add chilled sugar syrup. Blend. Pour mixture into 4 large glasses. Divide ice cream into 4 portions and add to orange mixture in glasses. Garnish with mint leaves and serve.

Tropical Cocktail
1½ cups fresh orange juice
1½ cups fresh grapefruit juice
½ cup fresh lime juice
Sugar if desired

Mix orange, grapefruit, lime juice and sugar in pitcher. Chill. Makes 6 servings.

Cranberry Punch
½ gallon cranberry juice
½ gallon pineapple sherbet (see recipe this book)
1 quart ginger ale

Chill all ingredients. Combine cranberry juice and sherbet. Put in punch bowl, then pour ginger ale slowly down inside of bowl. Makes 30 servings.

Party Punch

4 cup sugar syrup
1 cup lemon juice, strained
8 cups pineapple juice
2 quarts ginger ale, chilled
1 small can pineapple rings

Use recipe this book to make syrup. Combine syrup, lemon juice and pineapple juice. Chill. When ready to serve, pour into punch bowl. Add chilled ginger ale (from bottle), pouring slowly down inside of punch bowl. Float pineapple rings on surface of punch. Makes 30 servings (punch cups).

Fruit Milk Shake

2½ cups fruit juice
(either grape, berry, orange, or pineapple)
3 cups milk
1 teaspoon lemon juice

Chill juice and milk. Add fruit juice to milk in blender, then 1 teaspoon lemon juice and blend until smooth. Serve cold. Serves four to six.

Pot of Tea

1 teaspoon tea leaves per cup of water

Heat teapot by boiling water and pouring a little boiling water into the pot, swishing it around, and then out into the sink. Place tea leaves in a strainer in the heated pot. Pour measured amount of boiling water over measured amount of tea. Let stand 3 to 5 minutes until desired strength has been reached. Serve tea in china cups or in mugs. Enhance taste with sugar, slice of lemon, or milk. For a spiced tea, add 1 teaspoon cinnamon to pot immediately after adding the boiling water to tea leaves.

Iced Tea

Make tea per Pot of Tea directions. Let stand for 10 minutes or until tea is very strong. Add sugar to hot tea if sweet tea is desired. Add an equal measure of cold water then pour tea over ice in tall glasses. Add slice of lemon for flavoring if desired. Garnish glass with a sprig of mint.

Russian Tea

1 small can frozen orange juice
½ cup lemon juice
1 small can pineapple juice
½ cup sugar
1½ quart water
1 stick cinnamon
1 cup tea
1 cup ginger ale (optional)

Boil sugar in one quart of water, add cinnamon stick and simmer for five minutes. Cool. Add remaining ingredients with the ginger ale last. Serve hot or cold. Serves ten.

Hot Mulled Cider

2 quarts apple cider
½ cup brown sugar
1 teaspoon whole cloves
1 teaspoon allspice
1 teaspoon cinnamon
¼ teaspoon nutmeg
1 orange, sliced thinly and seeded

Combine all ingredients except orange into saucepan and bring to a boil slowly. Cover and simmer for 20 minutes. Strain to remove spices, then pour into mugs and add a slice of orange. Makes ten servings.

"Orange Julius"*
1 can frozen orange juice concentrate
1 cup milk
1 cup water
½ cup sugar
1 teaspoon vanilla
12 to 16 ice cubes

Combine all ingredients in a blender and blend. Serves six.
* Orange Julius is a trademarked beverage and I have no idea what the actual ingredients are. This is just my Mom's delicious brew that taste a lot like the Orange Julius we bought before the Saturday afternoon Roy Rogers movie in the 1950's. Goes great with a corn dog with mustard on it (you can find corn dogs in the frozen food section of your grocery store).

Harty-Party Punch
2 bottles Chablis or other dry white wine
½ cup brandy
1 cup orange juice
½ cup lemon juice
1 quart club soda
2 oranges
1 lemon
1 lime

Seed and thinly slice oranges, lemon, and lime. Chill all ingredients. Combine all ingredients and chill another 2 hours. To serve, pour into a punch bowl over ice. Add club soda and serve. Serves 20 to 30 (punch cup size servings).

MEASUREMENTS & CONVERSIONS

Liquid Measure
1 liter = 1.06 quarts
1 cup = 8 fluid ounces = 0.24 liters
1 pint = 2 cups = 16 fluid ounces = 0.47 liters
1 quart = 2 pints = 4 cups = 32 fluid ounces = 0.95 liters
1 gallon = 4 quarts, 8 pints, 16 cups, 3.79 liters

Dry Measure
pinch, dash, a few grains = less than 1/8 teaspoon
3 teaspoons = 1 tablespoon
4 tablespoons = ¼ cup
16 tablespoons = 1 cup
1 cup = 8 ounces = ½ pint
2 cups = 16 ounces = 1 pint
1 pint = 16 ounces = ½ quart
2 pints = 32 ounces = 1 quart
1 peck = 8 quarts
1 bushel = 4 pecks

Others
1 quart unsifted flour = 1 pound
2 tablespoons of ground spice = 1 ounce
1 ounce butter = 2 tablespoons
1 pound butter = 2 cups or 4 sticks
2 cups sugar = 1 pound
1 lemon = 3 tablespoons juice = 1 teaspoon grated peel
1 orange = 1/3 cup juice = 2 teaspoons grated peel
1 medium onion chopped = ½ cup pieces
8-10 egg whites = 1 cup
12-14 egg yolks = 1 cup
1 cup unwhipped cream = 2 cups whipped cream
8 ounces dry spaghetti = 4 cups cooked spaghetti

THANK YOU

We know you have many options for spending your money and we're glad you purchased this book. Visit our website, www.advancebooks.com, for information on other books you might enjoy and a schedule of author events.

ORDERING INFORMATION

Old-Fashioned Recipes for Modern Cooks
ISBN 0-9706224-0-6
$12 US Trade Paperback
November 2001 Publication

Splendor Bay, A Mystery
ISBN 0-9706224-1-4
$16 US Trade Paperback
December 2001 Publication

And More to Come

ADVANCEBOOKS books can be purchased through most bookstores, speciality stores, and gift shops. If not in stock, they can be ordered from national wholesalers by the store and you will have them in a few days. You may also order our books, including autographed copies, directly from ADVANCEBOOKS; however, orders requiring foreign shipment cannot be processed. For ordering information, email staff@advancebooks.com or visit our website, www.advancebooks.com.

COMING ATTRACTION!
WE ALSO PUBLISH FICTION
DECEMBER 2001 RELEASE
SPLENDOR BAY BY LB COBB
ISBN 0-9706224-1-4, Trade Paper, $16 US

Bill Glasscock, a suspended-for-malpractice attorney, wakes from girlfriend Sally Solana's bed to a crystalline May morning in Splendor Bay. Before noon, Bill faces the challenge of his life. The stiff the local cops have just found on the beach below Sally's bayview mansion is Governor Wallace Moreno, Bill's soon-to-be-ex-wife Eleana's lover. Sally, the state's attorney general, is missing. So is Eleana, head of the state archives. And, believe it or not, in addition to a complicated love life, Bill is the prime suspect of a host of cops—local, state, and federal. That's the catalyst Bill needs to abandon his sabbatical from life for a quest to save those he loves from a murderer.

Suspense, sensual and conflicted mainstream relationships, quirky characters you will love and remember, and wry humor are a few of the reasons *Splendor Bay* grabs you by the heart and sweeps you along on waves of emotions to its surprising conclusion.

Splendor Bay earned awards in the Tennessee Mountain Writers, Cumberland Writers, Faulkner Pirate's Alley, and SMP/Private Eye Writers of America unpublished novel competitions.

Advance Praise

"Smart, sassy, and sexy, with enough twists and turns to make you dizzy, Splendor Bay is a splendid read" — Lorna Michaels, author of *The Truth About Elyssa*

"Moral ambiguities, snappy dialogue, and twists that keep the pages turning... an exceptionally accomplished debut novel" — Chris Rogers, author of *Bitch Factor*

"A fabulous writer!"— Tony Fennelly, Edgar-nominated author of *Don't Blame the Snake*

"L.B. Cobb comes through with a page-turning story filled with cracking wit and suspense..." — Julie Wray Herman, Agtha- and Macavity-award nominated author of *Three Dirty Women and the Bitter Brew*

"The plot catapults with intrigue, quirky characters, and wry, wry humor"— Roger Paulding, author of *The Pickled Dog's Journey*